Kenneth Murray in his boat on Lagos Harbour, 1965.

This Book is Dedicated
to the Memory of
Kenneth C. Murray
1902 - 1972
Nigeria's First Surveyor of Antiquities,
later Director of the Federal Department of Antiquities

The Stone Images of Esiẹ, Nigeria

Phillips Stevens, Jr.

Ibadan University Press
and
The Nigerian Federal Department
of Antiquities

International Standard Book Number: 978 121 029 X
Library of Congress Catalogue Card Number:

Designed and Manufactured in the United States
of America by Harry Hoffman & Sons, Inc.,
Buffalo, New York

Contents

Foreword

The stone images of Esie have long been a mystery. The story of their origin told by the people of Esie expresses it as a mystery, for how could human beings turn into stone except by supernatural means? The people of Ife also tell stories of how, in the past, people were able to turn themselves into stone when death approached. In both places these stories reflect the fact that the technique of stone sculpture has been forgotten, presumably for a long time. Western scholars, however, have so far done no better in several decades of speculation. The origin of most stone sculpture in West Africa remains obscure, while an adequate way of directly dating stone sculpture has yet to be devised. The *nomoli* figures of Sierra Leone are conventionally dated to the sixteenth century because they resemble in style the Sherbro-Portuguese ivories which are more securely dated to that century. Most Ife stone sculptures bear little stylistic similarity to the better known terracotta and "bronze"-castings which can be dated; this is because the techniques of manufacture are very different. Stone sculpture is produced, like wood carvings, by a subtractive technique: the artist begins with a block from which he takes away the parts he does not want. In contrast, terracotta and bronze sculpture are produced by an additive technique: the artist adds more and more clay or wax in building up his sculpture. The style of the finished works thus tends not to be comparable. The only scientific dates we have from Esie are derived from fragmentary terracotta sculpture whose temporal association with the stone sculptures is far from certain.

The images of Esie are especially important for they are the biggest group of stone sculptures made on such a large scale to survive from the African past. More than eight hundred of them are still in Esie despite a number of thefts. They are thus an extremely impressive sight, even after they had been brought into a building forming an octagonal courtyard, built specially to protect them, the setting in which I first saw them in 1957. The sheer massing together of these pieces cannot fail to impress.

Dr. Stevens undertook to catalogue and photograph all these pieces as a Peace Corps Volunteer working with the Department of Antiquities of the Federal Government of Nigeria. He was able thereby to attain an unmatched knowledge of them which he makes available to the rest of us in exhaustive detail in these pages. He has carefully examined the various parallels which have been suggested in the decades since they became known to the world outside of Esie, only to reject most of them. Nevertheless he is able to suggest a hypothesis of their place of origin, which happens to be one of the places first suggested soon after their discovery (more as a guess than on a basis of evidence) but now he ties it in with our increasing knowledge of the history of Nigeria derived from the detailed study of oral traditions.

One feature of the style of these sculptures which I find especially interesting is the habit of representing major parts of the subject (not simply ornamental details) by incision — the feet are often incised into the stool on which the figure sits. I cannot recall any other style of African sculpture which shows this same mixture of techniques.

Dr. Stevens rightly draws attention to the fact that the female figures are commonly armed with machetes. It seems very likely that this has a symbolic significance. A recent study (not yet published) by Zdenka Volavka of the mother and child figures of the Lower Congo, often called ancestor figures, or in the French literature *maternités* and associated with fertility, suggests that they are in fact representations of political power. The women of Esie may well be the vehicles of similar symbolism.

Now that this important body of material has been made available we may look forward to its being studied by others who may be able to bring light to bear on it from other areas or disciplines. Nonetheless, these figures will retain their antique mystery for a long while yet.

Frank Willett
Hunterian Museum
University of Glasgow

I first saw the Esię stone images in February of 1964, on a brief trip away from my Peace Corps teaching post in Ibadan. I could not have guessed then that I would become so deeply and personally involved in the search for a resolution of this great mystery.

It was the policy of the Peace Corps that Volunteers be accountable for all but two weeks per year of their tours of duty. I spent my school holidays in service to the Federal Department of Antiquities, first filing and cataloguing in the Nigerian (now National) Museum, Lagos; later documenting antiquities in Ibadan and in outlying villages. During this time I became acquainted with the Department's Director, Kenneth C. Murray, who was delighted to receive unpaid help. Acting on petitions from both of us, the Peace Corps agreed to my transfer to the Department, and at the end of the 1964 school year I began full-time ethnographic work under Murray.

After a frustrating and relatively fruitless month of surveying what few active shrines remained in northern Ekiti and southern Igbomina areas, I was assigned by Murray to Esię, to catalogue and photograph the entire collection, and to effect what repairs were possible. I began work in Esię in late February, 1965, and spent most of the next 17 months there.

That was a rich and transforming period of my life. I have endless anecdotes of experiences during that time, but what remains strongest is a feeling of accomplishment, the more rewarding because of the graciousness of the people of Esię. After some initial — and quite understandable — confusion as to my purpose there, the people afforded me unqualified encouragement and hospitality, expressed in the nickname they conferred upon me, Eréwùnmi, "the images are pleased with me."

By the time of my departure in July 1966, the images and all significant fragments had been photographed and catalogued, the old crumbling structure sheltering the images had been demolished, two of three permanent museum buildings had been constructed, and the entire collection had been moved either to the new gallery for exhibition or to the storehouse for safekeeping and possible further repairs. Shortly afterward a third building, to be used as a workshop and, eventually, a second exhibition gallery, was completed, and an altar was built so that the people could continue their worship of the images through the figure designated as the "King."

I had by this time more than 3500 negatives and five binders of long-hand notes. Murray allowed me to bring these back to the States for further analysis. We had the idea of a publication of some sort, but this idea was not to materialize during Kenneth Murray's lifetime. He was able to see one of his visions realized; the documentation and provision of security for the images. Unfortunately he could not see the results of this research finally appear in print. He was killed in a road accident in April, 1972. My association with Kenneth Murray changed the course of my life. It is to his memory that this book is respectfully dedicated.

I entered into graduate study in anthropology and was able to work only sporadically on the Esię material. I returned to Nigeria to conduct my dissertation research from September 1969 through March 1971, but in an area quite far from Esię, both in distance and in focus. It was not until the end of 1973 that I was able to turn again to this material, and my relative freedom from other commitments coincided fortuitously with an expression of interest by the Ibadan University Press.

The Press wanted to publish the book to coincide with the Second World Black and African Festival of Arts and Culture, originally planned for November and December of 1975. Time was suddenly pressing. But I had found that some gaps existed in my data, and that some new photographs were desirable. I returned to Esię in July and August of 1974, and took another 1000 photographs and conducted additional research. The postponement of the Arts Festival gave me much-needed extra time. Ibadan Press had decided to have the book printed outside of Nigeria, and the printing firm of Harry Hoffman & Sons, of Buffalo, was selected. This allowed me the unique opportunity to be available for consultation throughout all stages of production; but the staggering magnitude of the job, coupled with certain unforeseen difficulties, delayed publication, and very unfortunately the book could not appear in time for the re-scheduled Festival in January and February of 1977. But it was for the Festival that this book was composed, and I hope it will be received in the Festival spirit of renewed enthusiasm for the traditional and contemporary arts of Africa.

The purpose of this book is twofold. First, to bring together all that has been ascertained and conjectured about the stone images of Esiẹ and the apparently related images in the nearby villages of Ijara and Ofaro, to evaluate the various suggestions, and to offer some of my own. Space is also devoted to discussion and representation of the several fragments of the little-known terra-cotta sculptures associated with the stones. This constitutes the text of the book. Second, to compile a catalogue of the images. This is accomplished in the Plates section.

The material set down here represents the culmination of twelve years of concern with the Esiẹ problem. It is a problem with which I have become personally involved, and very possibly my objectivity has been clouded as a result. My excitement has not waned, but I think it is long past time for me to bid a final farewell to Esiẹ and its images. I am hopeful that further investigations by geology and archaeology will support my concluding hypotheses, but the reader need not accept the interpretations I have drawn and the suggestions I have offered. Moreover, the book leaves many questions unanswered; indeed, it generates some new ones. But one aim in bringing all this material together has been to provide a useful tool for any who might wish to conduct further research into the great mystery of Esiẹ.

One set of questions left unanswered regards the actual production of the images: how many carvers are represented? Over how long a period of time were the images sculpted? It was my hope to be able to tackle these questions, and others, through a computer-based statistical correlational analysis of the various categories of features, weights, and measurements. A beginning was attempted, but for many reasons such an analysis could not be completed. Here is one possibly fruitful area of research that need not await further investigations in the field. The categories I arrived at are briefly discussed in the Introduction to the Plates, but they are too numerous and contain too much data to be included in detail in the captions. I will retain these data in the event that some future researcher might wish to use them.

Orthography

Yoruba words in the text are rendered according to most of the tenets of currently preferred orthography. Thus ẹ and ọ appear instead of the International Phonetic Alphabet symbols ɛ and ɔ, and ṣ represents the diphthong sh. In the representation of tonal marks I have not always been consistent, but I have tried to indicate them in most cases, including the proper names for supernatural beings, but not including personal and place names. In all cases only high and low tones are marked; mid-tones are left unmarked. Vowel length is, with a very few exceptions, not indicated; this is the only departure from established Yoruba orthography.

Acknowledgements

I am indebted to a great many persons for their contributions to the completion of the work which led to the publication of this book, but properly acknowledging their assistance is surely the most difficult task of all, for to try and mention all inevitably means neglecting some. But I must try, and extend my heartfelt thanks,

for seeing to many aspects of my welfare in Esiẹ, to: H. H. Jacob Oyeyipọ, Fifteenth *Elesiẹ* of Esiẹ, and Ogunniwun Ajokẹ, *Àwòrọ* of the cult of the images;

to some of the many who laboured with me at Esiẹ: Bakare Adebiyi, Jide Afolayan, Adebisi Amusa, Busari Bojuwoye, Elias Okoraike, Michael Oladipọ, Samuel Ọlaniyi, Isaac Olu, Henry and Barbara Wesselman, and students of the International School Ibadan;

for invaluable technical assistance at various stages, to: Ekpo O. Eyo, Phyllis Ferguson, Stephen Hoffman, Ottomar H. Pfersdorff, Thurstan Shaw, Robert Soper, and Frank Speed;

for accommodation in 1974, to: Frs. Michael Conboy and Dan Macauley, S.M.A., Catholic Mission, Oro;

for financial support of my 1974 research, to: The American Philosophical Society and the Research Foundation of the State University of New York;

for their assistance in promoting the 1974 research, to: Philip Allison, William Bascom, Robert F. Thompson, and Frank Willett;

for drawing the maps and printing nearly all of the photographs, to: Gordon J. Schmahl;

and for reading the manuscript and offering valuable criticisms, to: Philip Allison, William Bascom, and Frank Willett.

I am especially grateful to the following, who patiently saw the book through the long and sometimes painful stages of its production: Robert P. Armstrong, formerly Director of the Northwestern University Press; Ekpo O. Eyo, Director of the Nigerian Federal Department of Antiquities; Richard Hirsch, Vice President, Harry Hoffman & Sons Printing; and N. J. Udoeyop, Director, Ibadan University Press.

Special thanks go to my long-time friend and mentor, Frank Willett, for his wise counsel over the years, and for writing the Foreword to this book.

My wife, Susanna, and my children, Jeremy and Rebecca, endured disrupted evenings and weekends for a good many months prior to the publication of this book, and to them I can only express my loving gratitude.

Several persons who provided information at various stages are acknowledged in the text, or in footnotes. To those others who have had a hand in this work, but whose help I have not specifically acknowledged, I offer my apologies, and my thanks.

Photographic Credits

Several persons generously provided photographs, which appear as Figures, as follows:

I.1, p. 2   Charles Uht, for the Museum of Primitive Art, New York; supplied by Susan Vogel

I.2, p. 2   E. H. Duckworth; supplied by Philip Allison

I.4-10, pp. 4-7   H. V. Meyerowitz; supplied by Eva L. R. Meyerowitz

III. 1-5, pp. 32-34   Samuel Osifoluke; supplied by the Nigerian Federal Department of Antiquities

V.1, p. 50   The Nigerian Federal Department of Antiquities

V.7, 8, p. 56   Frank Willett

V.14, p. 60   Frank Willett

V.24, p. 67   K. C. Murray

V.25, p. 71   Herbert M. Cole, from *African Arts/Arts d'Afrique*, II, 3, Spring 1969, p. 9

All other photographs, including all the Plates, are my own.

Fig. V.29, p. 78, was kindly drawn for this book by the technical staff of the Department of Archaeology, University of Ibadan.

P.S., jr.
Buffalo, New York
July 1977

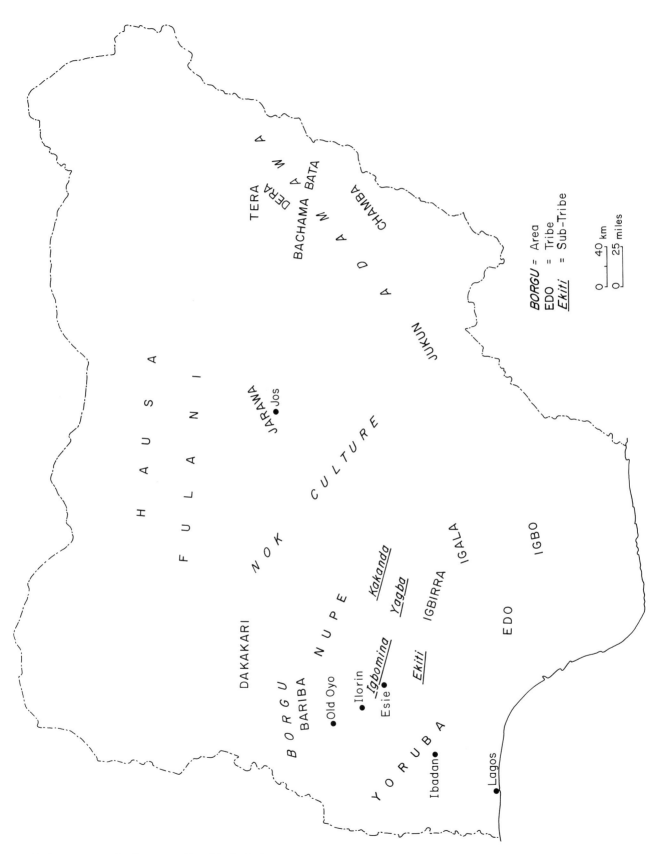

Map I. Some areas and cultures mentioned in the text.

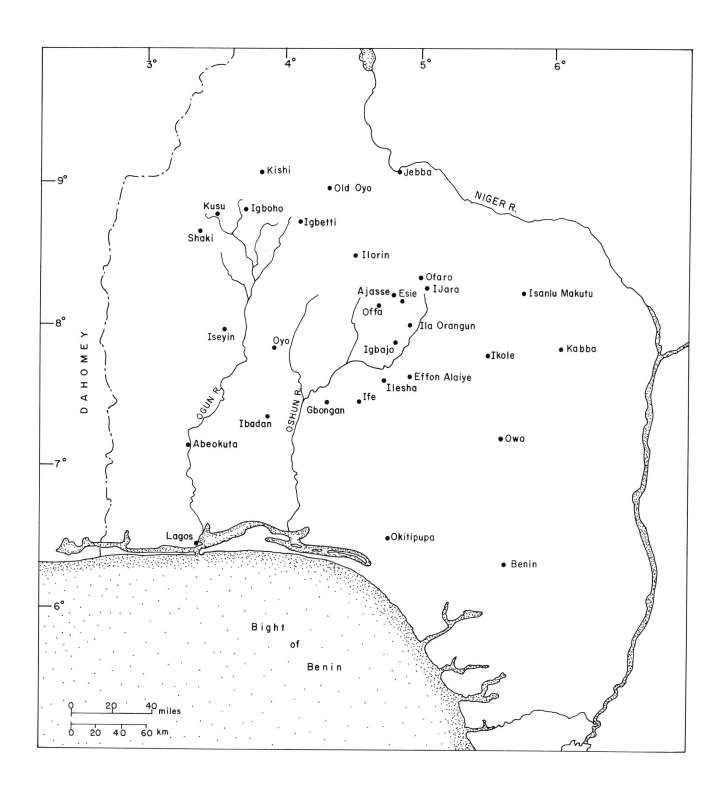

Map II. Some towns mentioned in the text.

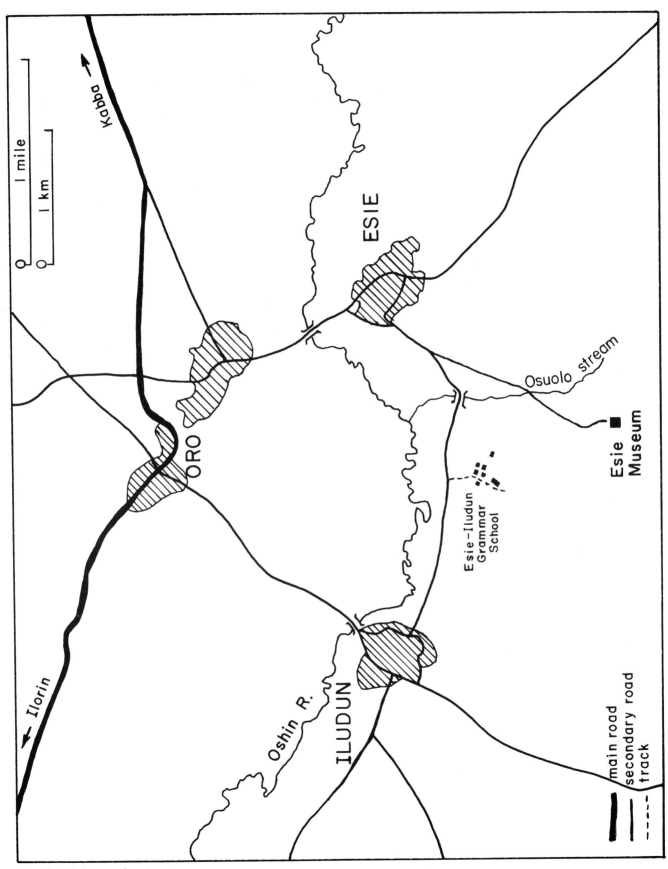

Map III. Esiẹ town and environs.

I

Background

In a sacred grove a little over two kilometres south-west of the Igbomina Yoruba village of Èsìẹ́ is a group of perhaps 1000 carved soapstone figures representing men, women, children and animals. "The Stone Images of Esie," as they have come to be known, constitute what is by far the largest collection of stone carvings in Africa, and their origins are one of the continent's great mysteries. They range in height from 14 cm. to over one metre. Most are seated on stools; a few are standing. Some are apparently reveling, laughing, playing musical instruments; most are stern; many are armed, as if for war. Their features suggest a diversity of influences, but they are all presided over by a "king," whose features have become nearly obliterated by the caked blood of countless animal sacrifices. Esie tradition holds that the statues are the petrified remains of visitors from a distant land, and they have occupied a central place in local cosmology, perhaps since the latter part of the eighteenth century when, according to historical tradition, the Esie people arrived at their present site.

Every year throughout the reigns of fifteen successive Chiefs of Esie, a cult with an established priesthood has celebrated a festival for the images. The festival is one of the most important of the year for the people of Esie and several near-by villages, all of whom have come to regard the Èrè (images) as owners of the land and principal overseers of the general welfare. At different times throughout the year, supplications, accompanied by sacrifices, are presented to the images, through the Àwòrò (Ayarun in Igbomina dialect), or chief priest, from local residents as well as from Igbomina who had emigrated to Ibadan, Lagos, Kaduna, and even more distant cities. It has been reported (Meyerowitz 1943:31; Oyinloye 1953) that even the Emir of Ilorin was aware of the responses and directives of the images, as interpreted through the Àwòrò's rituals of divination. Thus it is curious (although, in light of their subsequent treatment, perhaps fortunate) that the existence of the images became known to the outside world only as recently as the 1930's.

Leo Frobenius, the widely-traveled German expeditionary and anthropologist whose narratives of his adventures are often tantalizingly incomplete, in 1912 collected three heads in the Esie style. One (fig. I.1) found its way into the Helena Rubenstein collection, and is now in the Museum of Primitive Art, New York. In *The Voice of Africa* (1913) Frobenius advances his argument that the fine objects in bronze, terra-cotta, quartz, and granite of the "Classical Period" of Ife could not have been of African manufacture (he seeks an Etruscan origin); later African craftsmen preferred the more tractable medium of soapstone from which they produced crude copies of the ancient objects, "and one is struck with their coarseness and African clumsiness, tastelessness and lack of distinction" (p. 318). Possessed of such sentiments, he has only this to say about his Esie-style finds:

1

Excavations I undertook in the district of Offa allow me to state that there, too, in recent times, that is, about the Dutch period, stone images were manufactured ... The accompanying plates [facing p. 322 in *The Voice of Africa*, vol. I] bear witness to the fact they show the greatest partiality for dressing the hair and ornamenting it as fantastically as it might be, exactly as happens with the Benin bronzes of the same period. They are, however, so poor and degenerate in form as to possess no importance as works of art, but may well serve as documentary evidence of decadence in steatite shape.

Of his "excavations in the district of Offa," we are told no more. In any case, he most probably did not visit Esie; in spite of his purblindedness, he could not have helped but be impressed.

In spite of his denigrations, Frobenius' publication of his Offa finds might have spurred further investigation. That it did not may perhaps be attributed to the relatively sporadic conduct of anthropological investigations in Nigeria during the colonial period, as Jones (1974) has recently noted. In any case, the first European to "discover" the Esie figures was H. G. Ramshaw, Schools Inspector for the Church Missionary Society, in 1933. He was directed to the site by Rev. Fr. A. Simon, S.M.A., mission school-master for Esie and Oro, and founder of the Catholic mission at Oro. It is supposed that Father Simon himself never saw the figures, but had been informed of their existence by the local people.

During the same year Ramshaw directed a number of other visitors to the shrine, four of whom published accounts of the images (Milburn 1936, Daniel 1937, Clarke 1938, Murray 1951). When seen by Ramshaw, the grove was surrounded by dense foliage and the images themselves, as F. Daniel notes, "were overgrown with rank grass" (1937:43). Fig. I.2, taken by E. H. Duckworth, is the only photograph I have been able to secure of the state of the images in the year of their discovery. This shows the Àwòrò addressing the "King" of the images (Ọba Èrè, fig. I.5). For others taken during this period the reader is referred to Daniel's 1937 article.

I.1. One of three heads "excavated" by Leo Frobenius in 1912, 21 years before the sacred grove of Esie was known to the outside world. Museum of Primitive Art, New York. Ht. 30 cm.

I.2. The Àwòrò presenting his salutation to the King of the Images, 1933.

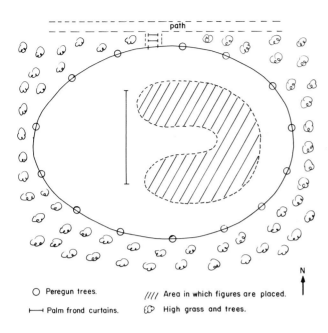

○ Peregun trees.　　　//// Area in which figures are placed.

⊢—⊣ Palm frond curtains.　　⟨⟩ High grass and trees.

I.3. Schematic sketch of the site in 1936 (after Daniel 1937:44).

J. D. Clarke notes,

At the time of their discovery the figures were crowded together with no attempt at arrangement and many were half-buried in the soft soil. The vast majority had either been decapitated or had suffered some dismemberment, giving the impression that they have at some time suffered from an outburst of iconoclasm, possibly Mohammedan ... more than half the figures had been reduced to fragments or completely defaced ... (1938:106).

Bertho and Mauny (1952:109) state that the statues were "obviously the objects of intentional damage." Indeed, a great many have deep cuts and gouges about the face and upper body, more than could have occurred by accident. It is certain that little, if any, of such destruction had occurred at the hands of the people of Esie. Some heads had been replaced on torsos (often mis-matched), and the king was periodically anointed with the blood of sacrifices, but otherwise the images were seldom handled. Most were heavily encrusted with lichens. Many had been covered by earth to a depth of from 30 to 45 cm., and when I first visited the site in 1964 a few of the figures still bore the dried remains of roots that had grown

thickly between their legs. When the grove was discovered it was completely encircled by pèrègún trees (a species of Dracaena), commonly planted around Yoruba sacred places, and the images were seen to have been placed in a rough semi-circle, with the king in a central position. Esie people assert that this was precisely the way they found the grove.

Clarke and S. Milburn were thus apparently the first persons in a very long time to alter the character of the grove and the positions of the images. They cleared away the grass and brush and unearthed some of the figures. Members of the cult hung palm-frond curtains before the images and at the entrance to the grove (also a common Yoruba means of designating sacred places). Fig. I.3 shows a schematic sketch of the site in 1936 (from Daniel 1937:44). Figs. I.4-10 show the grove and some of the images as they were photographed in 1937 by H. V. Meyerowitz.

In 1937 a shelter was erected to protect "the best of the figures" (Clarke 1938:106), apparently under Clarke's direct supervision (Meyerowitz 1943:35; Oyinloye 1953). A number of other images, and fragments of some small terra-cotta figures, were found during this process.

These renovations, however, could be effected only after a series of patient negotiations with the Elesie (Chief of Esie), Sunmonu Abikoye, and his people. Olatunji Oyinloye, a native of Esie, notes:

The ère are regarded as the most sacred gods of Esie. They are believed to be capable of giving children to barren women and of supplying rain whenever the town is in need of it. This accounts for the resentment to the publicity which the images have attracted. At first the people would not hear of any suggestion that the images be protected by a shelter. They stated that as they had been in the open since time immemorial, any attempt to cover or move them would bring disaster on the town (1953:14).

And even for the next 25 years visitors to the site were not warmly welcomed.

The shelter collapsed in 1944 because, according to Oyinloye, the people were unwilling to maintain it. The Government then intervened; the Secretary of the Northern Provinces authorized the Resident of Ilorin Province to urge the people to allow the images to be removed and permanently housed. The reply was an adamant refusal. In October the District Officer conferred in person with the Elesie, who asked for a few days to consult with his councillors. A schoolboy painstakingly drafted the Elesie's final reply, a portion of which is recounted by Oyinloye:

It is the wish of all the people of Esie that not a

single one of their images be removed because:

1. Yearly, all barren women go to the images to pray for children, and do succeed.

2. It is the custom in Esie̩ that people go to the images to pray for rain if there is no sufficient rain in a year.

3. Elesie̩ and his people are living at Esie̩ for the sake of the images, and if even one of them is taken away they will emigrate to the place whence the image is removed.

The next plaintiff was the Emir of Ilo̩rin, who visited Esie̩ with most of his royal retinue in November, 1944. The *Elesie̩* remained adamant in his decision. The Government decided against the use of force, and, according to Oyinloye, the Resident informed the Secretary that "the battle of the images at Esie̩ has been lost." The government had no alternative but to provide protection for the images on their sacred site.

In 1945 an octagonal building of concrete and local lateritic stone, with roof of corrugated iron, was erected on the site. The structure was designed in impluvial style, with an open inner courtyard. The images and all fragments were arranged on tiers around the inner walls (figs. I.11-14). At one end an altar was erected, on which was placed the *O̩ba Ère* and certain of the images designated by the *Àwòrò* as attendants to the king (fig. I.15). The single entrance was covered by a heavy wooden door fastened with a huge padlock, the only key to which was entrusted to the *Elesie̩*.

I.4. The images in 1937, from the entrance to the grove.

I.5. The "King" of the images in 1937, streaked by the blood of sacrifices. He is sunk in the earth to a depth of approximately 30 cm. The figure holding the cutlass, left, is HT 1.

I.6. The Àwòrò prostrating before the King of the Images, 1937.

I.7. Some of the images, 1937. In the foreground, center, is HT 193. The head in the left foreground, facing left, is that of HT 15. The image with the large head in the background, facing away from the camera, is HT 215. By reference to the Plates, other images can be identified.

I.8. H 130 on a mis-matched torso, 1937.

I.9. H 530 on a mis-matched torso, 1937.

I.10. HT 236 in 1937.

I.11. Interior of the House of Images, built in 1945, as photographed in 1965.

I.12. Interior of the House of Images, 1965.

I.13. Interior of the House of Images, 1965.

I.14. The north-east corner of the House of Images in 1965, showing damage caused by insects, rodents, and erosion.

Subsequent visitors to the "House of Images" (*Ilé Ère*), as the building was thenceforth known, were obliged to first visit the *Elesiẹ*. A guide, usually a boy from the local primary school, was summoned and given the key; he accompanied the visitors on foot from the edge of town through the fields to the House of Images. In 1948 Bernard Fagg, Government Archaeologist stationed at Jos, provided the *Elesiẹ* with a large ledger in which visitors were to inscribe their names and affiliations.

The problem of security proved to be an increasingly pressing one, however. It is not known exactly how many images or fragments have been removed from the site, but the number is considerable. Bertho and Mauny (1952:109) state that "more than 600 heads detached from the torso were discovered." Since the time of these early investigations several more heads have been found, but the total count in 1965 was 552. A great many of the severed heads were small enough to fit in one's pocket. So fragmentary are the images that the precise number of once-complete figures can never be known, but correlations of head-to body-size would suggest that perhaps 80 of the smaller torsos have necks too small to fit any of the loose heads which were still at the site in 1964-66. When the site was cleared and some excavations carried out in the 1930's under J. D. Clarke's direction, a number of fragments of terra-cotta figures were found (Daniel 1937:46), including several complete heads of people and animals; many of these have also disappeared.

Entries in the visitor's book showed that, by 1965, far fewer than 200 people had visited Esiẹ in any one year. But many of these must have succumbed to the tremendous temptation presented by the shelves of hundreds of loose heads and fragments. And pocketing one or two presented no problem; although the guide was usually enjoined by the *Elesiẹ* to carefully observe that none of the pieces were handled, what could a schoolboy say to a group of several adults? Most often he preferred to sit outside the *Ilé Ère* until the visitors were prepared to leave.

The problem was not unique to Esiẹ, of course. The Nigerian Antiquities Service, as it was known until Independence, had simply too small a budget to enable it to cope adequately with the tremendous task of control and regulation of the increasingly rapid flow of antiquities across Nigeria's borders, in re-

9

sponse to the expanding market for African art objects in Europe and America. The problem was compounded by the increasing number of new finds, and by what has been rather unsatisfactorily labeled "the missionary attitude:" the tendency on the part of recently converted peoples to ignore, destroy, or offer for sale their formerly venerated relics.

Almost alone in the struggle for preservation of Nigeria's antiquities and objects of traditional art stood Kenneth C. Murray, Surveyor of Antiquities since the late 1930's, and Director when the Department of Antiquities of the Federal Ministry of Education was established after Independence, until his retirement in 1968. Murray's tragic death in a road accident in April, 1972, occasioned a memorial issue of the journal *African Arts* (XVI, 4, summer 1973); the reader is referred to this for a partial recounting of the activities of this tireless ally of the arts of Nigeria.

Murray constantly worried for Esie. In 1957 he sent a team of Antiquities Officers, led by Chief Justus Akeredolu of Owo, to carry out as extensive a survey of the site as possible. A great number of the images were numbered and photographed, and some repairs were effected. Chief Akeredolu, assisted by Mr. H. K. Rashid (now of the Jos Museum) and Mr. Osula (currently at the Benin Museum), dug a number of test holes at various points around the site. Some new figures were recovered during these excavations, and the piles of fragments were increased. They worked on and off for more than 3 years. Rashid was thereafter stationed permanently at Esie until my assignment began in February, 1965. I worked there for most of the next 18 months. The methods and procedures followed in this work are discussed in the Preface and in the Plates section.

I.15. The King of the Images and some of his "attendants", in the House of Images, 1965.

10

During these months the progressing decay of the House of Images became increasingly rapid, as insects and rodents undermined the walls. I recall being startled from my work on two occasions, as a settling of the shelves caused an image to topple and break. The figures were further subject to harm from the curious hands of visitors. And whereas participants in the rituals had apparently not handled the images when they had occupied the grove, during these later years the principal focus of ritual activity became the Ọba Ère; the other images were shifted about, even used as stools, by the devotees.

The alternative to further theft and damage was clear. Toward the end of 1965 an architect, Mr. Lyczkowski, designed a new museum complex for Esiẹ (fig. I.16). During the dry season of 1966 the first two buildings, an exhibition gallery and storehouse, were constructed (figs. I.17-23), under the direction of Clifford Duxbury. The "House of Images" was demolished. The complete figures, those which we had been able to repair satisfactorily, and a number of the heads and torsos were placed on exhibition be-hind railings. The others were removed to the store-house. A permanent staff of attendants was employed at the site. Over the next three years a third building was constructed (fig. I.24), to be used either as another workshop, or a second exhibition gallery in the event that further repairs and reconstruction might be effected in the future. A sheltered dais for the Ọba Ère and a few figures selected by the Àwòrò as attendants to the Ọba was erected at the east end of the museum complex (fig. I.25), on the original site of the images and the spot on which the old House of Images had stood, so that the now few adherents to the cult could continue to observe their rites.

The labourers involved in the museum construction had build a service road from Esiẹ to the site; this road was widened and graded and now provides direct access to a spacious parking area in front of the museum. The site was landscaped and planted with flowering shrubs and various species of citrus and *Croton* trees. Final improvements were effected in time for the official opening of the Esiẹ Museum in 1970.

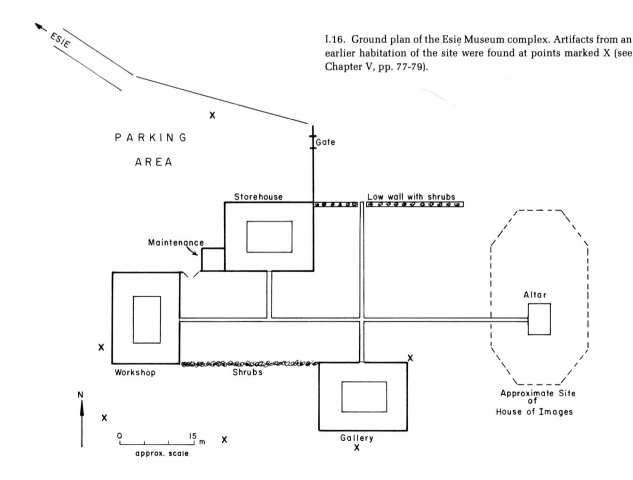

I.16. Ground plan of the Esiẹ Museum complex. Artifacts from an earlier habitation of the site were found at points marked X (see Chapter V, pp. 77-79).

I.17. The exhibition gallery, in need of re-thatching.

I.18. Looking east, past the storehouse (l.) and gallery (r.) to the altar.

I.19. View of the interior of the exhibition gallery.

Security was still not guaranteed, however. Sometime between the construction of the Museum and my return in July, 1974, the only complete terra-cotta head (TC 1) was stolen from the storehouse. In April 1974 a thief, demonstrating careful timing, entered the museum grounds from the yam fields behind the altar of the King during the brief early morning period when the nightwatchman had left and the day staff had not yet arrived, and made off with one of the Ọba's attendants (a very significant figure; HT 273). Supervision at the museum was increased to round-the-clock attendance, and as this book goes to press a high iron fence to surround the entire compound is planned.

The Esiẹ Museum is an impressive complex, and is today a major tourist attraction. The images, carefully and symmetrically ordered behind their railings, bathed in filtered light from Perspex panels in the roof, stand in mute tribute to whatever highly-developed and artistically-sensitive culture it was that produced them. Visitors, even restless children, invariably find themselves moved, their voices involuntarily hushed to whispers, their attitudes respectful, even reverent. One simply cannot remain unaffected. Even during my most intensive periods of work at the site in 1965-66, I very often found myself gazing, enthralled and transfixed, at one or another of them.

Detractors of museums have called them necessary evils, the mausoleums of dead or dying cultures. The mud-and-thatch construction of the Esiẹ Museum clearly provides a far more satisfactory home for the images than one of concrete, plaster, and glass. But, if one reflects upon their original surroundings, a bit of the sense of which is conveyed in figs. I.4-7, one must agree with Eva Meyerowitz' (1943:36) sentiments regarding the first structure on the site:

To the neat, museum-minded person the result no doubt is satisfactory, but from an aesthetic point of view it is a tragedy; for it has once and for all ruined a dramatic effect which will never be forgotten by those who, coming out of a narrow bush path, were suddenly confronted with this awe inspiring spectacle of an assembly, petrified and grotesque, within the vastness of the tropical forest.

13

I.20. Interior of the exhibition gallery.

I.21. Interior of the exhibition gallery.

I.22. Interior of the storehouse. The drawers, right, contain limb fragments.

I.23. Interior of the storehouse.

I.24. Looking west from the altar, past the gallery (l.) and the storehouse (r.) to the workshop.

I.25. The new altar for the King and selected "attendants". The altar stands on the site of the former House of Images. Some of the sacred *peregun (Dracaena)* trees can be seen in the background, left.

I.26. The new altar for the King. The bells described by Daniel (1937:44; see Chapter II, p. 23) lie at his feet. The small soapstone container, centre, was found in the rubble of the House of Images. The kneeling image, HT 270, is the only originally-designated "attendant" to remain with the king; for security purposes, the smaller objects were moved inside.

II

The Images in Esiẹ Cosmology

The people of Esiẹ are of the Igbomina sub-grouping of Yoruba, whose members constitute the great majority of the population of Igbomina Division, Ilọrin Province. Most Igbomina hold traditions of having emigrated, apparently in successive waves, from Old Ọyọ (Katunga),[1] the former Yoruba capital which, after a long decline, finally collapsed at the hands of Fulani invaders in about 1837. Migrations of those who were to recognize themselves as Igbomina possibly began as early as the mid-sixteenth century when Ọyọ was conquered by Nupe; this, and other events in Ọyọ history which hold possible relevance to our study, will be discussed further in Chapter V. The Olomu of Omu-Aran, a Grade II Chief, is recognized by Igbomina as their paramount ruler.[2]

Esiẹ Historical Traditions

The *Itan Esiẹ* ("History of Esiẹ"), an incomplete manuscript penned in Yoruba in the early 1950's by one Idowu and kept in the palace of the *Elesiẹ*, gives a sketchy, traditional account of the founding of the town. With some elaborations which shall be noted, the gist of this document was corroborated in testimony obtained from several Esiẹ elders; Oyinloye acknowledges it as having supplied the historical background for his thoughtful manuscript, "Esiẹ Stone Images" (1953).

According to the *Itan*, the royal clans of Esiẹ are descended from one Agbọnbifa, who left Ọyọ when Abiọdun was *Aláfin* ("the master of the àfin," palace; the title of kings of Ọyọ), in about 1670.[3] Agbọnbifa emigrated with his followers and "some Igbomina ọbas, because of shortage of land." They settled briefly at a place called Igbo-Eki, which they found unsuitable because of an unreliable water supply. They moved on to Okodo, now uninhabited, about seven kilometres northwest of Esiẹ.[4] There they stayed under Agbọnbifa and two successive chiefs, Orogbesasa and Okinkosefiniwo. The next chief was Baragbọn, a renowned hunter who was wont to spend many months in the bush. The water supply at Okodo had gradually proved inadequate to meet the needs of the growing population, and during one of his excursions Baragbọn came upon the stream called Osuolo (which flows about 200 metres from the site of the images), which he followed until it met the Ọsin, a larger stream which today separates Esiẹ from Oro. He went back to Okodo and informed his people that he had found a forested place[5] with two sufficient streams which would provide water the year round. Baragbọn, according to the *Itan*, brought his people to the present site of Esiẹ in about 1770.[6] Baragbọn is buried in Oke-Sanlu ward; an elaborate edifice, with a plaque to his memory, has recently been built over his grave (fig. II.1).

II.1. The grave of Baragbọn, Oke-Sanlu ward, Esiẹ.

II.2. The Hon. Jacob Oyeyipọ, fifteenth *Elesiẹ* of Esiẹ.

Following the death of Baragbọn were four successive *Elesiẹ*s, all of whom received their appointments from Ọyọ: Ọba Keke, Alaikosin, Ayoledoye, Elemele Ayaki. The *Itan* unfortunately gives no dates for the reigns of these rulers. It is tempting to surmise that the accession of the next *Elesiẹ* Iti Ajado, the first to be appointed from Ilọrin, approximately correlates with the demise of Ọyọ. But the decline of influence of the Ọyọ Empire had been long and steady, and by the time of its collapse it exercised virtually no external authority and had few allies. Ilọrin had usurped most administrative authority from Ọyọ several years before the fall of the kingdom; in 1820 that city was the headquarters of the famous Afọnja, the *Arẹ-Ọna-Kakanfo* or senior military leader, whose revolt against the *Aláfin* in about 1817 gave the Fulani a secure foothold in Yorubaland (cf. Johnson 1921; Ajayi and Smith 1964, and other histories).

All successive *Elesiẹ*s have been appointed from Ilọrin: Ọlarinde, Ọlayinka, Momoloso, Ifadọlapọ, Alufa, Ọlaṣupọ, Oyedokun, Sunmọnu Abikoye Fadọlapọ II, and Jacob Oyeyipọ (fig. II.2), the current holder of the title. Sunmọnu Abikoye is the first *Elesiẹ* to be positively associated with the images, from the accounts of their discovery cited in Chapter I. We can only wonder whether Baragbọn might have had any association with them; the *Itan Esiẹ* makes no mention of the images at all.

The Legends of the Images

In all of Esie tradition, in fact, there is nothing to suggest that the people had anything to do with either the manufacture of the images, or their conveyance to their sacred grove. On the contrary, all traditions assert that the images "arrived" considerably later than the founding of the town. We have only a number of legends, portions of which will be recounted in this section. Some of these contain elements which research has suggested might bear careful scrutiny and comparative investigation; such elements will be discussed in Chapter V.

Several variants on the legend of the images have been recorded. Elements have clearly changed over the generations; the presence of diverse elements in variants recorded during the same time period are generally due to the informants' genealogical or cult affiliations. Indeed, which version is considered the "right" one at any given time may be the one preferred by the clan of the person who holds the position of *Ayarun*, the priest of the cult of the images. Slight variations obtain in neighbouring villages as well.

The version most widely held today is that the images were originally people from many different tribes who had converged for some reason and had come together to Esie in search of a place to settle. Variations of this account refer to the migrants as "pale-skinned" (*òyìnbó*), and that they came "from the north." The version recorded by Milburn and published by Daniel (1937:45) says that the people "called themselves 'Yawa' and came from Egypt," stopping at Ife before moving on to Esie. The visitors camped in the fields outside the town and sent a message to the *Elesie* (he is never named) saying that he and his people should remain at home to receive them. After some days the *Elesie*'s senior wife exhorted him to think about his family and go and tend his okra crop, which might spoil for want of attention. He did so, and after his work on the farm he stopped to bathe in the stream near the edge of the village. While he was bathing the visitors came, and greeted him in passing (a variant says that they passed him still on his farm, and greeted him, "e kú isé o," "greetings on your work"). He realized his social blunder and hastened by a back path to the palace, entering it from the rear. When he came out to the front reception area the visitors had already been waiting for some time, unattended and in the hot sun, and they were indignant. The *Elesie* apologized for having detained them, but his story of having been inside preparing some refreshment for them was belied by an incriminating piece of okra leaf which still clung to his cheek. The visitors left, enraged, and returned to their camp.

They were subsequently turned to stone, by what agency and for what reasons differ from version to version. Daniel's account says that the visitors cursed the *Elesie* in the name of Èsù (the often-malicious trickster deity). This is a powerful and dangerous curse; Olórun (the Supreme Being) considered it unwarranted and turned them to stone. Daniel cites this as the origin of a saying, which must have passed out of usage — I never heard it:

> Omo ère kúnlè; kò rí eléjó
> Ó tu gbégi hánu.

My translation and interpretation are a slight revision of Daniel's: "The child of the images (the Elesie) knelt (apparently either to receive their curse, or in supplication), but he did not recognize his accusers (for they had been turned to stone), so he plucked a piece of *gbégi* (a grass-like plant) and put it in his mouth" (as one might casually chew a straw).

Other accounts say that following their disappointment at the palace the visitors returned to their camp in the fields, whence for some time afterward they harassed the villagers, until Olórun finally intervened, and turned them to stone. Devotees of Sàngó (the powerful god of thunder) or Ògun (in charge of iron and warfare) claim the act was the work of their patron deities.

Another version, held by adherents to the cult of Atankoro, a local spirit, claim the petrifaction as his doing. Once a powerful warrior and knight-errant, Atankoro wearied of his role and retreated to a hill about three kilometres to the west of the site of the images, where he lived as an eccentric recluse. His cattle (the short-horned dwarf cattle, called *enlá*, sing.) were accustomed to drink daily from the stream, Osuolo. He began to notice that occasionally one or two of them failed to return in the evening. On one occasion one of his animals returned home wounded by an arrow, and shortly died. He saw that the arrow was of foreign manufacture, and recognized it as belonging to the strangers in the fields. He went to them and confronted them with the arrow, demanding recompense. They responded with rudeness. Atankoro was a powerful sorcerer; he summoned his powers and turned the people to stone.

A variant of this legend accounts for the fragmentary state of most of the images. The belief in Esie, held by many today — and part of their stated rationale for their active worship of the images—is that even in their stony state the images are capable of malicious deeds, they "run about at night," and many mishaps are attributed to them. And so, it was after they had been turned to stone that they began killing Atankoro's cattle; he went to them in anger and struck and damaged many.

Harold Courlander, in his *Tales of Yoruba Gods and Heroes* (1973:143-6), offers a peculiar variant of the legend, a version of which I received no suggestion in Esiẹ: the town originally was a large and industrious metropolis, its inhabitants skilled in a variety of crafts and professions. "In a far-off country there were white people with great powers of medicine" who decided to visit Esiẹ, and sent word that they would be coming on a certain day. The appointed day, the message said, was sacred to these people, and no work should be done then. The Esiẹ people were reluctant to desist from their work, even for a single day; moreover, this was the time of year when daily attention to the crops was imperative. The story alleges that the Yoruba day begins with the rising of the sun; therefore, the people decided to perform their accustomed tasks before the dawn. But by dawn the visitors had already arrived. They indignantly informed the people that the day begins long before the dawn; therefore they had violated the sanctity of this day by working. The strangers summoned all their powers of sorcery and turned all the inhabitants of Esiẹ to stone. Later migrants to the area established a new town, discovered the images, and began an active worship of them.

The Cult of the Images

The images are actively worshipped by a cult whose members often refer to themselves as *àwọn ọmọ ère*, "the children of the images." Membership in the cult is acquired in ways similar to those governing entry into the worship of most Yoruba deities (*òrìṣà*): revelation by Ifá (the divination oracle) that such worship is necessary to avert or make amends for some misfortune; following the granting of a particular wish or prayer presented to the deity; or by having been "born into" the cult; i.e., one's lineage has customarily participated.

The cult is headed by the *Àwòrò (Ayarun*, in Igbomina dialect), the generic term for any priest. Formerly the *Awòrò* was a member of the *Elesiẹ's* compound, though not of his clan; he was apparently descended of slaves or others who had been adopted

into the royal family but could not inherit through the royal line. These were personal assistants to the *Elesiẹ*, and as such one was appointed by him as his representative; because of his initial offense, the *Elesiẹ* himself can never visit the images, nor even set foot on their land.

Subsequently the *Àwòrò* was appointed by the chief from his own clan. Since the time of Baragbon, three royal clans have formed from branches of the royal line: Fadọlapọ, Ọlayinka, and Momolọsọ. The first is Jacob Oyeyipọ's clan, and that of Ogunniwun Ajokẹ, the present *Àwòrò*. She is the second woman to have held the title. The first was one Eretoye, whose name means, roughly, "the images are sufficient for a titled office." It is not known who was *Elesiẹ* during her time. Ogunniwun succeeded Salami, who quit the position on accepting conversion to Islam; his predecessor was Ogunniwun's father, Abọsunrin Olumankan. At the time of Milburn's visit (Milburn 1936; Daniel 1937:44) the *Àwòrò* was named Idowu; it is apparently he who appears in figs. I.2 and I.6.

The *Àwòrò's* major duty is to conduct the annual festival of the images, although he is "on call" throughout the year, and may consult the *Ọba Èrè* during any crisis or important event. His only compensation is in periodic gifts from the *Elesiẹ*, or from individual supplicants. Personal supplications normally are made during the annual festival, but can also be conveyed through the *Àwòrò* at any time. During my tenure at Esiẹ, 1965-66, on two occasions offerings of a goat were sent by Esiẹ businessmen and traders resident in Lagos, accompanying requests for success in their business ventures. The images certainly seem to have smiled on businessmen in the past; Igbomina are frequently traders, and those of Esiẹ and Oro have been markedly successful. Both the large and impressive mosque at Oro and the Anglican Church of St. Michael at Esiẹ (fig. II.3) were constructed and furnished entirely with private funds; both villages boast a number of three- and four-storey private residences; and recently local businessmen pooled their resources to provide an efficient street-lighting system for Esiẹ.

Traditionally Esiẹ residents worshipped a number of "national" Yoruba *Òrìṣà*, notably Sàngó, Ògun, Obàtálá (the Creator, also called *Òrìṣà-Nlá*, "the great òrìshà;" cf. Stevens 1966), Òrìṣà-Oko (goddess of agriculture), Ọsanyìn (medicine), and others; and the *Egúngún* (the ancestral spirits) festival was a large yearly event. But the images have clearly dominated Esiẹ cosmology. Like other African sacred images, they are "fertility gods;" women who owe conception

II.3. The main road through Esie, looking south. In the foreground is an Antiquities Department sign (lacking a directional arrow, which should point to the right), guiding visitors to the Esie Museum. In the background is the Anglican Church of St. Michael. Funds for the electric street-lighting system were provided by local businessmen.

of children to them predominate in the cult's membership, and as we shall see below, they are also held responsible for a great measure of the general welfare.

The Annual Festival

The annual festival of the images (Odún Ère) has changed somewhat over the years. I cannot account for the deletion of some elements and the addition of others; they may, like the regard for a particular legend, reflect the preference of the incumbent Àwòrò. Daniel (1937:44-5), citing Milburn, describes aspects of the worship as follows:

On arrival at the entrance to the grove the Aworo strikes his bells [two clapperless bells, agogo, now kept on the altar of the Oba Ère] and advances slowly, crying 'Oluwa mi, Ago!' (My

Lord hail!). This greeting is repeated in quicker time as he approaches. When he reaches the figures, the Aworo bows before one in the centre [the king] and prays thus: 'Oluwa mi, a ji re? O ma dabobo gbogbo temi' [My Lord, what of your waking? Did you wake well? You are able to preserve all that is mine] . . .

The Aworo is not afraid of entering the grove because he has his bells to ring. Sometimes the figures appear to him in his sleep, and tell him that such and such a thing is going to happen.

The grove is the centre of a fertility cult . . . An annual festival known as Odun Ere is held in the dry season about Christmas time.[7] Drums are beaten in honour of the figures, and they are propitiated with offerings of kolas and the sacrifices of goats and fowls. On the second day a feast is held before Elesie's house. He is expected to provide suitable offerings, and the young girls sing songs about the figures:

Ere Elesie ebora die ko
E yawa wo ere; ere njo.

23

The figures of the Elesie are
  no small gods
Come and see the figures. The
  figures are dancing.[8]

Both men and women are allowed to enter the grove and wander round it and attend the yearly festival. The only prohibition is that the Elesie is not allowed to look upon the figures. If he were to see them, he would die.

Following is a description of the festival of the images as I witnessed it in 1965.[9] The festival takes place six days after the Egúngún festival; that year it began on the 29th of March. It lasted for three days. In the morning of the first day the Àwòrò and her many devotees, all women, danced and sang about the town. Swaying slowly, they chanted in a lilting rhythm the single phrase:

Ọmọ akèrè pọ mo eégun.

We are the children who bring together the
  images and the egúngún.

Meanwhile other women prepared great basins of food: ínyán (pounded yam), gàrí (cassava flour), èbà (cassava flour mixed with hot water to the consistency of coarse dough), a leafy vegetable called tètè, hard-boiled eggs, and palm oil. The ranks of the dancing group had been swelled by other townswomen, and they all, carrying the food, wended their way, still singing joyously, to the Ilé Èrè, the shelter housing the images, about two kilometres from the town. Several men joined the group, some carrying large pots, and one leading a tethered black goat. Other men went off to various places in the fields to prepare for the annual burning of the grass.

The party reached the shelter about noon. They stood outside for a moment, still singing, to announce their presence to the images. Then the women entered the shelter. The men remained outside and built a fire, laying out the provisions they had brought with them: salt, ground red pepper, and palm oil. Inside, the Àwòrò and her helpers carefully swept and cleaned around the central altar on which sat the Oba Èrè, the king of the images. They gently moved the kneeling attendants of the king to one side. The followers then seated themselves among the other images around the shelter, and the Àwòrò stood alone before the king.

She bent down and, addressing the ọba in a soft voice, offered the thanks of the people of Esiẹ for his having seen them successfully through the past year.

She explained that they had brought many gifts to him, and she asked for the guidance and protection of himself and the rest of the images for the coming year. She prayed for long life and prosperity for her own people who had been caring for the images these many years, and she asked the images' protection for the men who would soon begin the dangerous task of burning off the surrounding grassland. Finally she asked the ọba to accept the sacrifice and the food they had prepared for him.

By this time all onlookers had become silent. The goat was led in by three of the men, and decapitated on the ground in front of the altar. Some of the blood was collected in two basins; the rest was allowed to sink into the ground. The Àwòrò then poured the blood from one basin over the head and down the body of the king. She then took up a four-valved kola nut (obì àbàtà or obì gidi), broke it open, and cast the four cotyledons at the feet of the ọba.

Casting the kola is the simplest and most widespread means of divination among the Yoruba. During a religious festival it is advisable to cast kola at periodic intervals, to ascertain the spirits' responses to the proceedings. At this point in the festival of the images, the Àwòrò wished to know whether the ritual thus far had been conducted in a satisfactory manner, and particularly whether the king was pleased with the sacrifice, hence whether he was prepared to confer his blessings on the people. By the fall of the kola the ọba's response to the Àwòrò's supplications was divined in the following manner:

There are five possible combinations, each of which has a name in the Igbomina dialect. If three of the cotyledons lie with the inner sides down, and one faces upward, it is called òkànràn (literal meaning obscure). The appearance of òkànràn is greeted by great anxiety, for this is the worst possible combination. Nothing has pleased the ọba, and it is the job of the priestess, through further questioning and casts of the kola, to find out why he is displeased and what more he desires. If three of the segments turn up, and one down, it is iwà (manner, fashion), meaning that the previous proceedings have been acceptable, in this case the manner of the sacrifice, but that something more is desired. If all turn down (àṣíríbò — security) or all up (àláfíà—health, peace), the king is pleased. These are better combinations than iwà, but they indicate that something still is desired by the images. If two valves turn down and two up, this is the best possible answer, and is met by general rejoicing. This combination is called onyan (literal meaning obscure). If at any time during the ceremony any of the other four combinations turns up, the priestess must continue with more questioning, and perhaps another sacrifice, until *onyan* appears.

The *Àwòrò* bent down to inspect the fall of the kola (fig. II.4). Only three pieces were visible on the altar, two up and one down. The other piece had fallen behind another image. She summoned two of her followers, and they gingerly moved the image aside, exposing the wayward kola. It lay face down! She turned to the onlookers and announced, "*Onyan!*" Tense faces broke into smiles, and cries of "*e ṣé o!*" (thank you) and "*kábíyèsí!*" (a greeting to an *ọba*, from *Kí á bí ìyè si*—"let you have more life") signalled the happy ending of the first stage of the ceremony.

Then the food-bearers, who had been standing, somewhat anxiously, off to one side, picked up their several basins of food and brought them to the *Àwòrò*. She mixed portions of the *gàrí* with palm oil, and sprinkled the remainder of the goat's blood from the second basin over all the food. She then placed a handful of each of the various foods (except the *ẹ̀bà* and pounded yam) and one egg, on the *ọba*'s feet. After three casts of the kola nut she determined that the king was pleased with this offering. She then walked around the shelter, the basin of *gàrí*, palm oil,

and blood under her left arm and, in the manner of a sower of grain, cast handfuls of food to the other images. The remainder of the food, save the pounded yam and *ẹ̀bà*, which would be eaten later with the goat-meat stew, was passed around to the onlookers seated among the images. The *ọba*, the images and the people all partook of the same food at the same time.

Meanwhile the men had taken the goat outside. The carcass, together with the severed head, was laid over the fire to singe off the hair. This done, it was disembowelled and all parts were separated, thoroughly washed in water, and put into a large pot which had been placed over the fire. Pepper, palm oil, and salt were added, and the whole was left to simmer for two to three hours.

The first part of the meal having been finished, all participants and onlookers waited patiently, chatting among themselves, some walking from time to time to the altar to gaze silently at the *ọba*. Finally the stew was ready. It was poured out into a basin and carried to the *ọba*. The jawbone and some of the choicest pieces of meat were placed at his feet, together with portions of the pounded yam and *ẹ̀bà*, both of which had been warmed briefly over the fire. Some of the

II.4. At the commencement of the Annual Festival in the old House of Images, the priestess inspects the fall of the kola she has cast before the King.

soup was poured over the now considerable pile of food. A small basin of water was placed on the altar to one side of the ọba, so that he might have a drink after his meal (fig. II.5). More kola was cast; it was determined that the ọba was pleased, and that the people might join him in partaking of the goat. The ẹ̀bà, pounded yam, and stew were passed around, everyone taking a portion. In this way all the people participated in the sacrifice, and partook of the communal meal.

The first day of the festival was drawing to a close. In the cooling hours of late afternoon the men in the surrounding fields systematically set fire to the grass, assured in the knowledge that the images had granted their protection. All these fields within a radius of approximately one kilometre, it was explained, belong to the images; it is only through their grace that the grass can be burned off, hunters can have access to the wealth of small game animals and birds, and the new spring crops can be planted in the fertile soil.

As the crackling of the burning grass grew louder, and the white smoke billowed upward, the Àwòrò and her immediate followers donned similar plain blue wrappers, and knelt on the ground facing the ọba and bowed their heads to the earth. After touching their heads to the ground three times they rose and danced, single file, about the shelter, singing their songs of praise to the images. During the first circuit all the female onlookers joined in. After they had circled once the others retired outside the shelter, and only the immediate followers of the cult were left inside the Ilé Èrè, to complete two more circuits. They moved slowly and rhythmically, singing in unison:

Ẹbọra rere mà lère o
Èrè gbé wa yún, ere gbé wa bọ̀
Ẹbọra rere mà lère

Nígbà yí èrè kè jà
Kí lòkè nṣe?
Kí lodò nwò?

Ẹbọra rere mà lère, etc.

The gods which are good are the images
The images carry us going, the images
  carry us coming
The gods which are good are the images.

When the images do not quarrel
What is the hill doing?
What is the river looking at?[10]

The gods which are good are the images,
  etc.

When the third circuit of the House of Images was completed the women again knelt and bowed three times to the ọba (fig. II-6), and the first day of the festival was over.

The second day was devoted to rest and recuperation. No one at all visited the House of Images. The third day was reserved for those who had special requests to make of the Ọba Èrè, for those who wished to give thanks to him for having granted a request made the previous year, and also for any who wished to pay their last respects to the images before leaving them for another year. On the morning of this day only five women supplicants followed the Àwòrò to the shrine. They were joined by a small band of onlookers. Three of the women had come to make special requests; the other two were wives of the Elesie, who are obliged to come each year to pay homage for their husband.

The Àwòrò broke and cast kola, begging the attention of the ọba to the requests of the supplicants, who had knelt in a row behind her, and who were gazing steadfastly at the stern face of the image (fig. II.7). The first woman handed a fresh kola to the Àwòrò, saying, "Mo tọrọ ọmọ" (I beg for a child). The supplicant's eyes never left the image as the Àwòrò repeated the request and cast the kola. Onyan turned up. The woman clasped her hands and managed to utter, "A dupẹ o"(thank you) before falling down on her hands and face in gratitude. The other two women had also come to beg for children. Each presented her kola to the Àwòrò, and each intently watched the face of the ọba as if for a sign, as the wish was repeated and the kola cast. Onyan appeared also for the second woman; but for the third the terrible face of ọ̀kànràn turned up. What was the reason for this stern rejection? If the kola had proclaimed ìwà, àsíríbò, or àláfíà it would not have been nearly as serious, and perhaps the slight displeasure of the king could be appeased by the sacrifice of a cock or a pig, or even by a promise. The Àwòrò went on with further questions, interpreting the fall of the kola, while the unfortunate supplicant, close to tears, followed every query and response. No, no sacrifice was needed. Was it because of some offence against the èrè, or a particular òrìsà? This was possible, but probably was not the case. Was it because of some domestic strife? Yes. A quarrel with the husband? Yes. At last the Ọba Èrè gave the reason for his displeasure, through the interpretation of the Àwòrò. No more could be done. It was possible, the Àwòrò explained, that the images might relent, and sometime in the course of the year the woman

II.5. The King of the Images, after the sacrifice. Portions of food lie at his feet. The schnapps bottle contains palm oil.

might conceive. But for the present she had to face the prospect of going childless through the year.

Finally the wives of the *Elesie* came forward and offered kola and water to the *oba*, thanking him on behalf of the *Elesie* and his people for his guidance and asking for further protection and prosperity throughout the coming year. The final cast of the kola was favourable; the women knelt and touched their heads to the ground in a final gesture of humility and gratitude, and the Festival of the Images came to an end.

Ère gbé wa yún, ère gbé wa bò . . ." All aspects of the everyday life of the people are watched over, and controlled to some degree, by the images. The believers, therefore, must constantly be searching their souls and actions for any false step, for any possible way in which they might offend the images or their neighbors. Anyone could be called to task by the images for any social blunder, any misdeed, or any promise unfulfilled and, like the unfortunate woman doomed to remain childless for a year, face the displeasure of the images and the consequent denial of a special wish or desire. In this way all the people have at least a deep respect for, and many have built

their lives around, their own solution to the mystery of the Stone Images of Esie.

1965 was the last year the festival was conducted in this manner. The following year the cultists could focus only on the king and his few "attendants," as the others had either been removed to storage or lined up for photography, cataloguing, and repairs. Probably because of the temporary disruption caused by the accelerated construction of the new museum complex — the rains were not far off — participation in the festival was sparse. No suppliants at all appeared on the third day. In any case, because of the inroads made by Islam and Christianity and the values of modernization, the number of direct participants in the cult has been becoming increasingly smaller. The *Àwòrò* did, however, ascertain, through the fall of the kola, that the king was pleased at the prospect of a new, secure home for his subjects! Shortly thereafter the House of Images was demolished, and the images were assigned to the new gallery, behind a railing, or to the storehouse, under lock and key. Only the king and his attendants were left outside, on their special altar. I do not know how the cult has adapted its ritual to its new surroundings.

II.6. Members of the cult kneel before the altar and bow their heads to the ground.

II.7. The third day of the festival. The priestess divines on behalf of the supplicants behind her.

Notes, Chapter II

[1] As Allison (1968:23) has noted, Igbomina have effected adaptations to both savannah and forest environments. Those southern, forest Igbomina, whose largest settlement is the town of Ila-Ọrangun, claim an Ife derivation. This problem raises a possible question as to who the Igbomina actually are, which will be discussed further in Chapter V.

[2] Although Elphinstone (1921:11) states that the *Olupo* of Ajaṣẹ "appears to have been the most powerful" Igbomina chief.

[3] Agbọnbifa's name means "wise as Ifá."

One account asserts that all Igbomina are descended from Odùduwà, who established the first human settlement at Ife (cf. Stevens 1966). Oyinloye (1953) cites Lijadu's *Ifa Ipilẹ Esin Yoruba* (an undated booklet which appears in English translation as *Ifa, God of Our Fathers*), which contains the tradition that the original *Elesie* was the youngest son of Ọlọfin, a son of Oduduwa. Oyinloye adds, "If this is true, the title of Elesie must be very much older than 1670."

How this date, and that of 1770 for the migration from Okodo to Esie, were arrived at, is not clear. The *Itan Esie* does give the name of Abiodun as the Aláfin at the time of Agbọnbifa's exodus. But Akinjogbin (1967:175, n.1) has established Abiọdun's dates as 1774-1789. The name of Alafin Abiodun was widely known, and reference to him in the *Itan* may have been added for purposes of authentication. More likely, however, is the possibility that the wording of the *Itan* is confused. The history of Ọyọ *before* Abiodun was poorly known at the time the *Itan* was written, Johnson's *History of the Yorubas* (1921) being the most widely consulted source, and so the collapsing of history can be forgiven. But the subsequent testimony indicates that two chiefs ruled after Agbọnbifa, and *before* the people were led to Esie by Baragbon, the fourth in succession. And see n. 6, below. The chronology of the *Itan* would therefore be more accurate if it had reported, as Meyerowitz (1943:31-2) has, that the people *arrived* at their present site during the time of Abiodun.

[4] It was during July and August of 1974 when I pursued this line of investigation. This was the rainy season, and I was dissuaded from attempting to visit Okodo, which would have been overgrown. I was assured, however, that "many things" are to be found there, including potsherds, ridges and mounds indicating the layout of dwellings, slag and tuyères from smithies, etc. The place might bear archaeological investigation.

[5] This element in the legend supports Allison's suggestion (1963:94; 1968:23) that the area around Esie was formerly far more heavily forested than it is today. See n. 1, above, and Chapter V, p. 55.

[6] Enoch Afọlayan, Chief Petu of Esie and second to the *Elesie*, told me that the people had stayed at Okodo for 150 years (interview conducted August 6, 1974).

[7] It may be that Milburn was informed that the festival takes place "at the end of the year." In fact, as is common among African agricultural societies, the Esie year begins with the first rains.

[8] Indeed, an illusion of motion may have been created by the sun's rays, filtered through the trees of the grove. Unlike other African sculpture (cf. Thompson 1974), however, the images were surely not meant to be seen in motion; although many are easily portable, they were not handled.

This song is not sung today. Possibly it fell into disuse when the images were moved into their tiered shelter, where it would be difficult to imagine them "dancing."

[9] This section, with slight modification, is excerpted from my article, "The Festival of the Images at Esie," which appeared in *Nigeria Magazine*, no. 87, 1965; and is reproduced by kind permission of the editors of *Nigeria Magazine*.

[10] The meaning of the second verse is not clear. It could refer to the hill of Atankoro, discussed earlier, and the stream where his cattle were accustomed to drink; the hill is only about three kilometres from the site of the images, and the stream flows through their land. But any association of Atankoro with the images is denied by members of the ère cult. The people do believe that the images "quarrel," and that they are wont to run about the countryside at night, getting into mischief. These final lines, therefore, probably have a more general meaning: that when the images are content and at peace, all creation is also at ease.

III

The Images of Ofaro and Ijara

Soapstone carvings of the Esiẹ type have been found in two other Igbomina villages, Ofaro and Ijara. As these are held by local tradition to be associated with Esiẹ, we should consider them at this point. The accompanying photographs were made in 1974, hence they were not catalogued with the Esiẹ collection and do not appear with the Plates.

The Ofaro Pair

At the abandoned village site of Ofaro, some 35 kilometres northeast of Esiẹ and about three km. west of the present site of Owode-Ofaro, is a pair of soapstone images, male and female, partially sheltered by the V of two rock slabs projecting at angles from the ground (figs. III. 1, 2). It is not clear who first brought the images to outside attention. Phillip Allison (personal communication, 1974) thinks they were discovered by Donald Friend, "a wandering Australian artist who lived at Ikerre [Ekiti] for some months in 1939." Friend was interested in Nigerian stone carving, and published the first account of the Efọn Alaaye group (Friend 1939; Allison 1968:18, 20).

The earliest published account of the Ofaro stones, however, is Daniel's brief note (1939:107-8), from which I have extracted the following observations:

Under an overhanging ledge of rock are two stone figures, representing a man and a women . . . The villagers first stated that the figures were found in situ by their ancestors when they came to Ofaro many years ago.

Subsequent enquiry, however, elicited, the fact that the Bale [Baálè, from babá ilé, "father of the house," a lineage head] of Ofaro bears the title of Elesie and is a kinsman of the Elesie, village head of Esie . . . He informed me that his grandfather came originally from Esie, and it was he who first revealed the figures to the local inhabitants. In the light of this information there can, I think, be little doubt that the figures came originally from Esie. They have been sheltered from the weather by the overhanging rock and are now further protected by a grass roof built by the villagers. They are in charge of an Aworo or priest and periodical sacrifices are made in their honour, but as at Esie, the Elesie himself is not allowed to see them.

Further documentation was secured by Philip Allison, who visited Ofaro in March, 1960, and established the Ofaro pair as No. 33 in the list of scheduled Ancient Monuments under the Antiquities Ordinance. His report, filed with the Department of Antiquities, contains the following additional information:

III.1. The two images at Owode-Ofaro. Photographed 1974.

III.2. The Owode-Ofaro images.

They were said to have been brought from Esie before the time of the first Olu of Ofaro — the Olu I met was said to be the 34th. The day of my visit, 18th March, was the last day of the annual five-day festival called *Ajo Odun Ere*. On the previous days sheep, turkeys, fowls, and doves had been sacrificed to them, and on the day of my visit I was told that the hunters had gone out to get game for the evening sacrifice, the last of the festival. The images were sparsely spattered with blood, with a food offering of yam flour porridge on the rock before them . . .

I was never able to visit Ofaro, and no photographs of the images were known to exist. At my request Dr. Ekpo Eyo, Director of Antiquities, very kindly sent a photographer and ethnographer to the site in November, 1974. The accompanying photographs (figs. III. 1-5), the first of the Ofaro stones to be published, were taken by Samuel Osifoluke. The following descriptions are composed in part from notes made by Clement Oyeoka.

The images are partially protected by a fortuitous rock formation. Neither Allison nor Oyeoka made any mention of a "grass roof built by the villagers" which

32

Daniel noted in 1939. Each figure is 60 cm. in height; the head of the male measures 18 cm. from the shoulder. Each wears several string necklaces, and each has a bracelet on the left wrist. The female has a double hair band, but is otherwise unadorned. The male, however, bears elaborate scarification down its back (fig. III. 4) and has three vertical cicatrices at the back of the neck. These marks are identical to those on many of the Esię stones. Both stools are of the typical mushroom shape; that of the male has a spiral shaft. Judging from the photographs, little attention was paid by the carver to the feet of the female, which blend in with the base of the stool. The feet and toes of the male, however, are carved in high relief, and they appear to be considerably larger than the feet of most of the Esię figures. The female figure is slightly pitted and has lost its right hand. The exposed fronts of both are encrusted with lichens; otherwise they are in very good condition. The photographs show them as they are considered properly positioned, with the female to the right of the male.

Mr. Oyeoka notes:

Upon enquiry it was gathered that the first Olu of Ofaro, whose name the local people no longer remember, brought the images to the old site of Ofaro, now deserted. The Olu had come from Oke-Isanlu in Esię[1] with his entourage and all those who had favoured his cause in a civil strife. The local people know no more than this as to the origin of the Ere . . .

Allegedly, the Ere can spare toil and sorrow to those who have faith in them. They are said to watch their people — the local people of Ofaro — with tender care; but would, in return, accept sacrifices in the nature of blood spattered on them and food offerings placed on the rock before them. They are still being venerated. The worship of the Ere is general, for all and sundry, but it is forbidden for the Elesie or Chief of the community to see the Ere . . . The celebration takes place in March or April.

Yet, the Ere are found in an abandoned location, the old site of Ofaro. The area is a valley between two lofty hills, connected to Owode-Ofaro only by a bush path . . . Mr. Jacob Adebayo, aged sixty-five, claimed that old Ofaro was abandoned because the surrounding hills did not permit easy communication with the outside world . . . Today, only paw-paw, plaintain, and banana trees, and some features like the grinding stones and the debris of fallen ancient buildings — and, of course, the Ere — are evidence that the valley had once been inhabited.

III.3. The Owode-Ofaro images. Each is 60 cm. in height.

III.4. The male image, rear view.

The present *Olu* of Ofaro is pictured in fig. III. 5. Apparently he still bears also the title of *Elesie*, but the tradition of his ancestors having been related to the *Elesies* of Esie, from whence he migrated to establish Ofaro, is unknown in Esie. The present *Elesie*, Jacob Oyeyipo, said that he had been told that there were images "like the *ère*, in some other villages;" but none of my informants claimed any knowledge of Ofaro.

The Ijara Group

Neither do the people of Esie know specifically of the images at Ijara, some 23 kilometres from Esie, off a branch of the same road which leads to Owode-Ofaro.

Mr. Jack Leggatt of the Ministry of Works is credited with the discovery of these images, on April 2, 1962. His report to the Antiquities Department (Leggatt 1962) was filed on April 15th. Illustrated accounts were subsequently published by Slye (1962) and Allison (1963). I visited the site on August 4, 1974; the accompanying photographs are my own.

The figures stand atop a hill about 1½ kilometres south-east of the village. The sides of the hill are cultivated by local farmers. Round about the top and about one-third of the way down the sides of the hill the ground is littered with lumps of slag and fragments of clay tuyères, clear evidence of smithing activity. On the very top of the hill is a grove of trees under which, in a small clearing, stand the images, eight in number. They are arranged in a rough circle at the center of which a rather ornate pot has been inverted in the ground, its concave bottom appearing as a shallow dish.

In overall treatment the Ijara images compare with some at Esie — in the Plates section, see HT 3 particularly — but they lack the detail and ornamentation of the Esie stones. All are seated on the typical mushroom-shaped stools. Nearly all are fragmentary and in generally poor condition. They have not been

III.5. The *Olu* of Ofaro.

protected and are badly weathered and coarse in texture; it is this that persuaded Leggatt that they "are sculpted from local rock" and Allison that they are of "a light coloured crystalline rock whereas many of the Esie figures are of steatite." In fact, the Ijara figures are carved in steatite, a fragment of which was collected for analysis (see Chapter V, pp. 74-76). In his 1963 article Allison assigned numbers to the images. As their positions had been altered when I visited the site, I have re-numbered them in the captions to the photographs (figs. III. 6-14). For purposes of comparision, Allison's original numbering appears in parentheses preceding each description.

Ijara is governed by an oba, who presides over the neighboring village of Iji as well, and is chosen alternately from one or the other village. At the time of my visit the Oba resided in Iji; Ijara was headed by a baálè. The following notes were obtained from a gathering of elders at the Baálè's house. This information, with some elaboration, accords fairly closely with that recorded by Leggatt and Allison twelve years previously.

The people of Ijara know nothing of the origin of the images. They were unearthed accidentally by farmers after Ifá (the divination principle) had revealed to a babaláwo (lit. "father of the cult;" a diviner-priest of Ifá) that "there were gods nearby." After their discovery, Ifá was consulted again; these were indeed the gods mentioned, and the people should enter into their worship. The images were arranged in their present shrine, and they became the focus of a cult presided over by the babaláwo, who bore the title of Èsìnkin Awo (èsìn is worship, awo is cult or mystery). From him subsequent Àwòròs have descended.

Unlike the festivals for the images at Esie and Ofaro, the annual celebration for the Ijara stones is held in November, at harvest time, and is associated with the New Yams. The images themselves ensure fertility in women and preside over domestic and local affairs. The largest of the images (no. 4) is regarded as the most important, and is the one who receives the sacrifice, the nature of which is revealed by Ifá before the festival. The celebration lasts for just one day. In the morning the cult members and their following gather in the village and dance to the shrine, clapping and singing the single phrase,

> Ère kó omo wòlú

> These images have brought children
> into the town.

These notes have been phrased in the "ethno-graphic present;" active veneration of the images has long since been discontinued. Present-day attitude toward them is casual; it is not known whether they still possess the "great power" they once had. The present Àwòrò, by name Adewoye, has never performed the ritual. But he asserted that there must always be an Àwòrò, for in the event that someone "has a vision" the cult of the images might be reactivated.

Some of my informants had heard of the Ofaro stones; all knew that there were "many ère at Esie". As to the evidence of smithing activity on the hill of the images, all agreed that this was the site of a smithy established by "the people of Olowu," a powerful warrior-hero and blacksmith "from Esie." It was asserted that he did not bring the images with him, nor could any association between him and the images be ascertained. For further information about Olowu I was referred back to Esie.

The Legend of Olowu

The following account of the legend of Olowu is reconstructed from an interview with Enoch Afolayan, Chief Petu of Esie (cf. Chapter II, n. 3), conducted August 6, 1974. It must be acknowledged at the outset that no association between Olowu and the images of either Esie or Ijara can be positively established. But the story should be told, primarily because of the proximity of Olowu's activity areas to the sites of the images, but also because it will be seen to contain elements of interest to comparative folk-lorists, and it might never be related elsewhere.

Olowu's parentage is unknown. He was not an Esie man, although he was an Igbomina. He arrived in Esie at a time when warfare and slave-raiding were rampant. He was a wandering knight-errant, a brave warrior endowed with miraculous powers. He was also a blacksmith nonpareil; he forged all his own weapons and those of his troops, and it is said that if a piece of metal was lost in the fire he would plunge his arm up to the elbow into the coals to retrieve it. He assured the Esie people that he would always protect them from any external threat. He established his headquarters and central smithy at a place called Okiwo, not far from the site of the images. Fragments of slag and the remains of structures can be seen there today, just off the entrance road to Esie-Iludun Grammar School (see Map III).

III.6. The Ijara group, with the *Àwòrò*. No. 1 is the complete figure at left; others are numbered clockwise. No. 4 is approx. 60 cm. in height. Numbers in parentheses in the captions to figs. III.8-14 are those assigned by Allison (1963). A fragment of a tuyère lies on the ground just in front of No. 1. Photographed 1974.

III.7. Another view of the Ijara group.

After he had successfully defended the town in many battles, he summoned all the people to him and said that it was now his time to leave, he was needed elsewhere. He indicated a spot where an inverted mortar had been sunk into the ground. If at any time the people needed his protection, Chief Petu should strike the mortar three times with a pestle, while calling out Olowu's *oríkì* (personal praise-name):

Olówù, oyeye nimo, agbètù lówó ojoyìnbon!

Olowu, the powerful one, who snatches
gunpowder from the bumbling
incompetent!

Olowu warned the people that this was a serious matter; at no other time should they utter his *oríkì*, and only when in real need should they attempt to summon him. Then, there at Okiwo and in the presence of his people, he sank into the ground.

The people brought great quantities of palm-nut shells and spread them around the mortar so that he would have a ready supply of fuel for his forge. And thereafter he was summoned several times to go and meet some enemy or other. Each time he appeared he would seize a handful of sand and cast it upon the high grass; the stalks of grass would become soldiers who would instantly form ranks and follow him into battle. After the battle had been won the soldiers would disperse, not to be seen again.

While the Esiẹ people were still at Igbo-Eki (see Chapter II, pp. 19),[2] the people of Ora[3] (a place near Okiwo, now uninhabited) were living at Oruku. From there they went to Igbo-Afa, and thence to Ọra. After they had stayed sometime at Ọra, they held a great festival which went on far into the night and degenerated into unbridled debauchery. Some of them decided to test Olowu's power through the method entrusted to Chief Petu. Olowu appeared, called forth his troops, and asked who was the enemy he had been summoned to vanquish. When he realized it was a false alarm, his soldiers fell upon Ọra, and destroyed it and all its residents. Evidence of settlement can be seen there today.

Olowu was never called on again. Many generations after the destruction of Ọra, during the reign of *Elesiẹ* Oyedokun and Balẹ Ọdẹyimi, Olowu appeared in a vision to a certain man of Iludun who was instructed to take the following message to Chief Petu: the people of Esiẹ should worship him regularly, and on important occasions they should make a sacrifice of a mature she-goat and 200 eggs; on occasions of lesser importance they should offer a male dog or an adult male pig. In return for these attentions he would continue his military protection. And so Chief Petu and his line have conducted the worship of Olowu. Although since the cessation of warfare the people have never required his services, individuals have from time to time received visions in which he revealed certain requests, and they have continued to answer him.

III.8. No. 1 (1) at right; head with undecorated conical cap, broken off and replaced; left arm missing from shoulder to wrist; six-strand necklace. No. 8 (7) at left; right hand broken off (Allison says, "but preserved"; it could not be located when these photographs were made): four-strand necklace.

III.9. No. 2 (6). No head; right hand rests on knee, left hand on belly; four-stand necklace.

III.10. No. 3 (5). Trunk, legs and left hand only survive. A much-defaced head, with no obvious match, placed horizontally on the neck. When Allison visited the site, this head had been placed on No. 2.

III.11. No. 4 (3). Head with conical cap, plaited band, broken off and replaced; left hand missing; five-strand necklace.

III.12. No. 5 (2). No head; right arm and left hand missing; five-strand necklace.

III.13. No. 6 (8). Fragment; left leg and left side of trunk only.

III.14. No. 7 (4). Trunk, left hand, and legs only survive; four-strand necklace.

Notes, Chapter III

[1] This is interesting, as Oke-Isanlu is the burial place of Baragbon, the leader of the original migrants to Esie (cf. Chap. II, p. 19). I recorded no remembrance in Esie of any "civil strife" so severe that it resulted in one group's absconding with two of the sacred images. Oke-Isanlu is one of the original wards of Esie, and it seems more plausible that its name has become associated with the Ofaro images, which clearly show an Esie affinity, through a recent attempt at validating their presence. Allison, in 1960, had recorded a tradition that said the images were brought to Ofaro *before* the first Olu was installed. See Chap. V, n. 23.

[2] The chronology is obviously confusing. But, as in the cosmological systems of many peoples, the sphere of myth and legend very often operates parallel to, but without direct correlation with, the sphere of chronological "history."

[3] Who these people were is, of course, a mystery. Their association with "Oruku" and "Igbo-Afa," which places apparently do exist, serves to place them within a plausible historical framework. But it is probably best to regard the story of the people of Ora, and their Sodom-like fate, as allegory.

IV
The Terra-Cottas

Very little can be said about the fragments of terra-cotta sculptures and utilitarian items found in association with the stone images at Esie. These were first discovered by Milburn and Clarke in 1937, while clearing the grove for the construction of the first shelter (cf. Chapter I, p. 3).

They are not regarded as especially important by members of the cult of the images; indeed, few Esie people seem aware of their existence. Many of the terra-cottas have been purloined, and these thefts represent sad losses indeed. Daniel (1937:47) writes, "Certain terracotta fragments recently discovered include portions of two ornamented lamps, one in the form of a human head with mouth wide open to receive the wick and the other in that of a hedgehog with a hole in the back for the same purpose." Neither of these was in the collection when I began work in 1965, and no photographs of them are known to exist. The other known theft is that of the only remaining complete head, TC 1 (figs. IV. 1, 2), sometime between my departure in 1966 and my return in 1974. It is certainly this head Daniel is referring to: "The only link, beside their propinquity, connecting these fragments with the stone images is the fact that one of the terracotta heads has the same three lines behind the eye" (1937:47). He also notes, "There are also two small heads and some fragments of legs and lampstands." He does not indicate whether these two heads were complete; if so, they are gone. Fig. IV.3 shows the only fragments of heads remaining.

Details of some of the fragments show affinities with some terra-cottas found at Ife (see examples pictured in Willett 1967), but this is an inconclusive observation. Some limb fragments also resemble certain items of the "Nok culture" found on and near the Jos Plateau, and which have been dated to as early as the middle of the first millenium B.C. Frank Willett's excavations at Old Oyo in 1956-57 led to the discovery of a fragment of a terracotta head (Willett 1959b), but it shows no similarity to those four from Esie of which we have photographs. In fact, the features of the Esie terra-cottas, with the possible exception of TC 1, are not sufficiently diagnostic to link them specifically with any known tradition. The two larger head fragments in fig. IV.3 show partial facial striations, but as will be discussed further in Chapter V, attempts to reconstruct relationships on the basis of facial marks alone are inconclusive at best.

Daniel is quite right; we cannot be certain that the terra-cottas were produced at the same time as, or by the carvers of, the stone figures. On the other hand, there is no reason to suspect that they were not. The complete head (TC 1) and the upper half of a head (TC 2) bear strong resemblances in overall treatment to four (H 128, 244, 245, 545) of the six stone heads which were carved complete; i.e., were not connected to torsos. Two unidentifiable fragments were dated by thermoluminescence in 1974; the date of approxi-

IV.1. TC 1, stolen from the storehouse sometime between June 1966 and July 1974. Photographed 1965. Ht. approx. 11 cm.

IV.2. TC 1, side view.

IV.3. Head fragments. TC 2 is in the middle. The scale is in inches (near side) and centimetres.

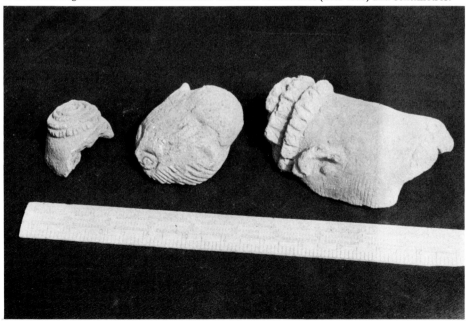

mately 1100 A.D. thus obtained is exciting, but again, inconclusive; its potential implications, and limitations, will be discussed in Chapter V.

Referring to the durability of terra-cotta, Willett (1959b:180) remarked, "It is likely . . . that the study of terra-cottas will be more rewarding than the study of any other form of sculpture in the study of art history of West Africa." Unfortunately, the Esiẹ terra-cottas will, at least for the present, have to remain a frustratingly tantalizing mystery — possibly even a mystery separate from that of the stone images. We can do no more here than to illustrate the most significant of them.

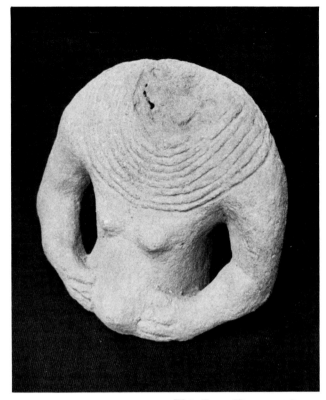

IV.4. Torso. Ht. approx. 9 cm.

IV.5. Miscellaneous torso and limb fragments.

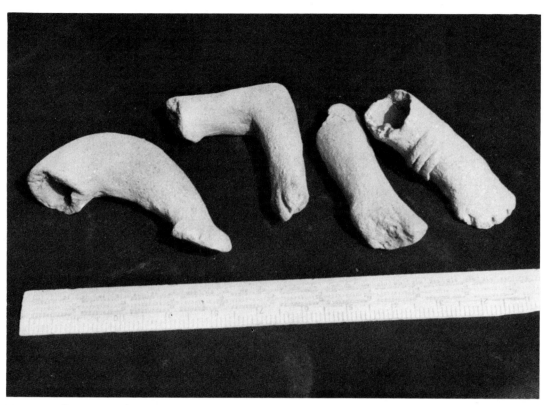

IV.6. Miscellaneous arm fragments.

IV.7. Miscellaneous leg fragments.

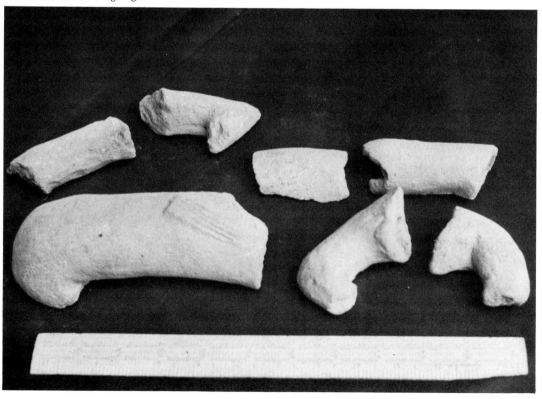

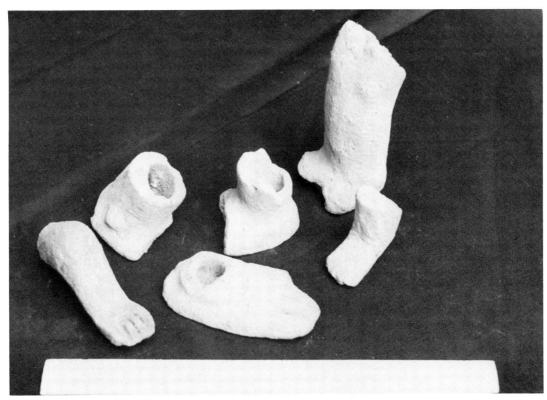

IV.8. Miscellaneous leg and foot fragments.

IV.9. Body of a male animal, probably a dog.

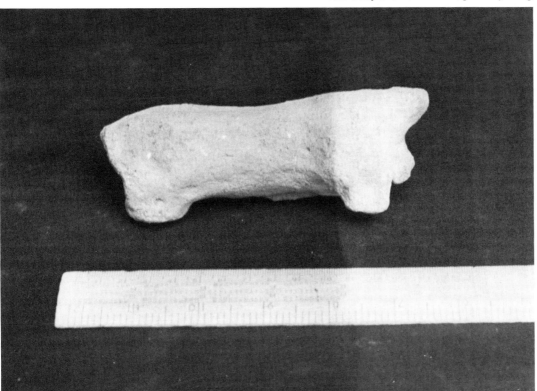

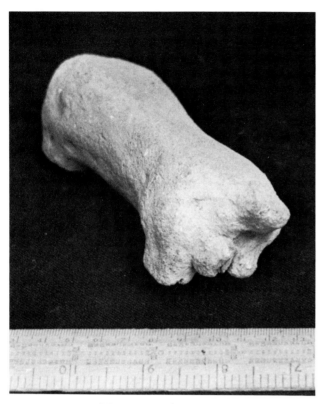

IV.10. Rear view of the animal in fig. IV.9.

IV.11. Pot stand. The design is continuous: three large openings near the top, three small ones near the bottom.

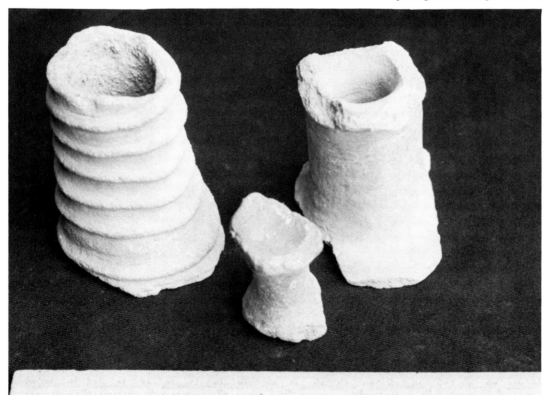

IV.12. The two larger fragments are necks of pots. The smaller one is a fragment of a handle, or perhaps of a pot-stand.

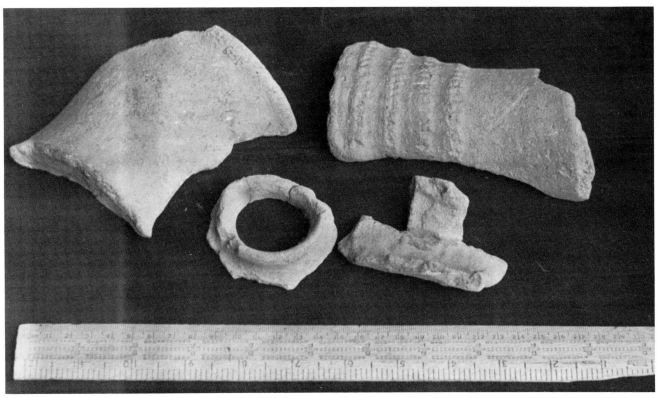

IV.13. Fragments of rims and necks of pots.

IV.14. Miscellaneous fragments.

IV.15. A small pot which had stood to one side of the King, on the altar in the old House of Images. It was used as a receptacle for offerings during the annual festival, and it is likely of more recent manufacture than the other terra-cottas.

V

Origins: The Great Mystery

The puzzle of the origins of the Esiẹ stone images represents what could surely be classified among Africa's great mysteries. That they were produced elsewhere, carried and deposited at their present site, there can be no doubt. But who made them? Where, why, and when? Why were they brought to Esiẹ, and by whom, and what happened to the people who brought them? Most of these, and the innumerable other questions that the Esiẹ collection generates, may never be satisfactorily answered.

I am certain, however, that we will, perhaps in the near future, have answers to some of these questions. It will be the purpose of this chapter to assess the present state of research into the resolution of the mystery, and to offer some conclusions as to which avenues of continued investigation might prove fruitful.

Suggestions as to the origins of the Esiẹ images fall into several categories, each of which will be briefly discussed and evaluated. Up to the present all such suggestions have been based wholly on conjecture and, to some degree, circumstantial evidence. These constitute what we might call "soft" data, and will be discussed — and, in the main, dismissed — first. Categories of such conjectural inquiry include evidence from tradition, comparisions with other artistic traditions, particularly of soapstone carving, and comparision of features seen on the Esiẹ stones with traits found among contemporary — and historic — populations.

Recently, however, some indications of "hard" data have begun to emerge. The second section of this chapter will present what I think to be a more reasoned use of traditional evidence, compared with historical data and bases for the potential roles of geology and archaeology. Throughout this section I will lean increasingly toward the notion casually suggested by some writers, but held consistently by K. C. Murray: that the area of the old kingdom of Ọyọ holds the greatest promise for a resolution of the mystery of the images.

Conjecture from Traditional Sources

Everyone who has ventured any thoughts on the origins of the Esiẹ images has been struck by the great range in variation in dress, accoutrements, and physical features represented. Although many of the figures show distinctly "negroid" features, most striking have been the "northern" elements. Caps on many have been likened to the fez; facial scarification, particularly the three parallel marks behind the eye, have been attributed to Nupe or other origins; decoration and style of weaponry, objects held, and items of dress, suggest northern influences. Some of the physical features are long and gracile, suggesting Hamitic origins; Clarke (1938:106) was struck by "the Northern type of face with swelling forehead, straight nose and pointed beard" — as, for example, represented by the reconstructed figure, H 348-T 95 (fig. V. 1). A few of the caps show what Milburn described as "an endless interlacing design common in local wood-carving and reminiscent of Celtic art" (Daniel 1937:47), as represented in H 188 (fig. V. 2); this pattern is widespread in Yoruba, Edo (Benin), and Nupe wood-carving, but is also common in northern embroidery and leatherwork. Some of the figures play the raft-zither, an instrument sometimes found in, but not indigenous to, the south, seen in T 104 (fig. V. 3). These are only a few illustrations of features which have been cited in support of theories of northern origins; some others will be referred to later.

Recognition of this great diversity, especially of the incidence of northern elements, is found first in the Esiẹ legends of origins (cf. Chapter II, pp. 21-22); all the variations have these elements in common: that the "visitors" were "people of many different tribes," "pale-skinned strangers" (northerners are generally lighter of skin; indeed, the term òyìnbó, commonly "white person," seems originally to have been applied to Hausa-Fulani), who came "from the North."

V.1. H 348 - T 95, illustrative of the Northern physiognomic features seen in several of the images. Ht. 78 cm.

V.2 H 188. The cap shows a decorative pattern widespread in the southern Sudan. Ht. 17 cm.

V.3. T 104, holding what appears to be a raft-zither. Ht. 54 cm.

Milburn recorded a version (Daniel 1937:45) which says that the people "called themselves 'Yawa' and came from Egypt."

During the first half of this century the notion of Egyptian or other Eastern origins of many of the nobler elements of cultures in the Southern and Western Sudan became increasingly popular. This notion was fostered in part by a general unwillingness to allow for the possibility of the independent development of Sub-Saharan civilizations, and in part by the fact that the traditions of so many West African societies place their origins to the east or north-east. But the attempts of many to extend these to Egypt or even further on the basis of certain assumed cultural and linguistic similarities have been fairly thoroughly discredited. Many such correlations have been shown to have been based on entirely circumstantial evidence, which in some cases has been selectively sifted to support premises held by their authors, or even on the wishful or merely fanciful thinking of their proponents.

Eva L. R. Meyerowitz, referring to the parallel marks between ear and eye on so many of the images, "which the people of Esie recognise as the ancient tribal mark of the Nupe," goes on to conclude flatly, "this, in my opinion, settles the tribal origin of these figures in spite of the fact that they are now standing on Yoruba soil" (1943:35). Frobenius (1913) had earlier concluded that the Nupe kingdom was founded in 641 A.D. by refugee tribes from Nubia. Meyerowitz summarizes his argument: "Persians who invaded and occupied Egypt in A.D. 619, and who were defeated by the Romans, fled into Nubia where they upset the local tribes and populations to such an extent, that a big migration took place across the Sudan. Many new kingdoms were founded in the course of time and amongst them was the Nupe kingdom which included part of the country along the Niger ... and also is said to have included, at one time, the Ife country and parts of Benin" (Meyerowitz 1943:35). She concurs with these sentiments, and finds support in the "Yawa" element in the legend recorded by Milburn:

> Nubia in the seventh century had many Yawa or similarly pronounced place names, there is Yerwa (Meroe) in Southern Nubia, Yafa in Maris in Northern Nubia, the people of which were originally Sabaeans and worshipped stars to which they erected idols. There is also Tafis or Tafa, sometimes written Yafa. The whole legend seems to contain a dim recollection by the Esie people that the ruling caste of the Nupe originally

came from Nubia and that some of the figures depict these pale skinned invaders.

We should note, however, that "Yawa" (properly, *yau'wa*) is the common Hausa expression of affirmation or enthusiasm, and that it is a widespread practice, particularly in areas where there is considerable inter-tribal contact, for one people to refer to another by an often-heard expression in their language. I found several instances of this during my researches in Adamawa,[1] an area comprising a great many small societies, some belonging to totally different language families. Thus, the "Kanakuru" (Dera) are so called because of their morning greeting; the Bachama and Bata are often called "Pompurom," from their first greeting; and a central group of Chamba chiefdoms was called the "Nyaganyare," from an expression meaning, roughly, "How do you do?" In his Yoruba dictionary, Abraham (1958:706) notes that the Hausa greeting, "sannu," also came to be used by Yoruba *(sanún)* and other non-Hausa, as the word for any Hausa person, in the same way that "the West African troops in the East African Campaign called the Swahili troops of the King's African Rifles by the name of Jambo, because 'jambo' in Swahili means 'how are you?'" I also heard some Esie people refer to Hausa as "Madalla," from the common Hausa expression meaning "wonderful!" (derived from the Arabic, "thanks be to Allah!").

The "big migration . . . across the Sudan" to which Meyerowitz refers, is most likely the alleged "Kisra migration," legends of which obtain among many Sudanic peoples, and which has been discussed at length by several scholars. Frobenius credited it with the introduction of a great many elements of apparently foreign origin into the southern areas. Daniel (1937:49), discussing a possible connection between the Esie images and Old Ọyọ, notes that Ṣàngó, an early king of Ọyọ before his apotheosis to the role of the all-powerful thunder god, "was by tradition an Ibariba of Borgu." He goes on,

> There is an ancient connection between the Yoruba of Ọyọ and the conquering dynasty of Borgu who claim descent from Kisra, the mythical leader of the Kwararafa migration. Whatever his true origin, Kisra seems to have come from the East, whilst the "pale strangers" of the Esie legend came from Egypt. Can the Esie statues be copies of work done by Eastern craftsmen introduced by Kisra's descendents?

Reference to the legends of Kisra by scholars aiming at demonstrating Egyptian, Arabic, Persian, or even more exotic origins of certain elements in sub-Saharan cultures gave their arguments additional support. There were, to be sure, a number of successive waves of influence across the Sahara, beginning even before the seventh century, many of which conveyed Persian, Arabic, and other elements. But I have elsewhere (Stevens 1975) recently reviewed the sources, both historic and traditional, and have concluded that, rather than by any specific migration, the *idea* of Kisra was brought across the Sahara by any number of migratory movements, as well as by merchants and traders. "Kisra" is derived from the Arabic form of *Khosrau*, the title held by two Persian kings of the sixth and seventh centuries. The most probable candidate for the referent of Kisra was Anushirwan, Khosrau I, who died in 579. He never entered Africa, but his fame as a strong but fair ruler extended throughout the Arab world; "Kisra" *(Kisrawî)* came to be equated with the sum of the noblest elements of royalty, universally worthy of emulation. The armies of Anushirwan's successor, Khusru Parviz (Khosrau II, d. 628) did enter Africa, and occupied Egypt for ten or twelve years until they were driven out by the Roman emperor Heraclius. But Parviz, an avaricious despot, is an unpopular historical figure; in any case, by the time of his reign, the notion of Kisra as the embodiment of noble values had already become widespread. Thus certain militaristic societies of the southern Sudan — such as Borgu — seized on "Kisra" and adapted the idea to the foundations of their mythologies of kingship.

Another speculation based on tradition has ignored the northern elements in the Esie legends, as well as suggestions of northern influences in the figures themselves, and argues for a southern origin of the stone images. This is an oft-cited account of "four hundred and forty idols" of Ikole, some 80 km. southeast of Esie, in Ekiti Division. This tradition was first recorded by Bovell Jones (1936), and was mentioned again by Meyerowitz (1943:35), Murray (1951), Oyinloye (1954), and Allison (1968:24), and was included in the brief statement of traditions which was inserted in the first Visitors' Book placed in the House of Images. As Jones related it, one Akinsale, son of Olofin and grandson of Odùduwà himself (cf. Chapter II, n. 3), left Ife with his followers and four hundred and forty idols. "Akinsale was told by Olofin that he should call himself the Alakole, because two hundred idols had been added to the two hundred and forty idols usually worshipped at Ile-Ife, and that the place in which he settled should be called Ikole." Jones concluded, "As far as we know no 440 figures or idols of any type have been found in Ikole, and it

seems highly probable that the Esie figures are the ones mentioned . . . unless somebody can prove the existence of the idols of Ikole." I think it probable that there were no such idols; rather that "idol" may have been a mis-translation of *òrìsà* (deity). An Ife tradition asserts that after the time of Odùduwá, 240 *òrìsà*, including most of the "national" gods with the notable exception of Sàngó,[2] were revered by the people. Allison (1968:14) relates a tradition that 401 *òrìsà* were recognized. An account I obtained (Stevens 1966) states that there were 201 local *òrìsà*, the Oni (king of Ife) himself being the 201st.

A final, and most interesting, speculation on the origins of the Esie stones is that more recently offered by Eva Meyerowitz. In a personal communication of December 1974, she writes, "I am now of the opinion that they are the work of the Asebu people who, refugees, came about 1400 to the coast of Ghana." Of the Asebu and their stone figures she has recently written (1975:85-6):[3]

> The Asebu who believe that they arrived on the coast after the Afutu had settled there came, according to their tradition, from "a place in the desert beyond Northern Nigeria." Presumably following a war they left and moved south into the Benin region and arrived at a time "when the tribes there were fighting each other." Avoiding them they finally settled south-east of Benin City in a country which is still named after them, Sobo. They lived there unmolested until the arrival of a people whose men wore thirty-two marks on their faces and their woman sixteen.

> Forced to leave they wandered into the Ife region . . . until ousted by a Moslem people who wanted them to adopt Islam. They moved to the coast . . . When they knew where they were going they constructed boats . . . The women, the potters, the carriers of their sacred stone figures, and the blacksmiths to whom the sea was taboo, walked along the beach.

> The Asebu finally stopped at the Etsi fishing village of Mowure (Moree) and built their first settlement nearby, a place now known as Asekyere Bedzi. Their leaders were two brothers, Kwegya and Amenfi, and their sister Amenfima. After a while Kwegya and Amenfima went inland, and on a little hill founded a small town which is now found at the bottom of the hill and called Asebu after its people.

> Amenfi, on the other hand, subjected the Etsi at Moree. The decisive battle took place on the path

leading from Moree to Asekyere Bedzi on the Bay of Moree . . .

The fallen Asebu warriors were buried in a grove on the beach. Over their graves, it is said, were placed the ancestral figures which the Asebu had brought from their former homes together with new ones portraying the dead, carved out of stone or in terra-cotta. Today the grove is covered by the sea and the hundreds of figures can be seen only at the end of December during the Harmattan season when the sea is dead calm and the water clear. The grove is now called Fonfrompomu, the Silent Grove, and at the annual festival the priest pours a libation to the dead from a boat at sea.

The Asebu were subsumed under the Akan after conquest.

Earlier (1952:66-7) Meyerowitz had described her own investigations into the mystery of the Asebu figures; in 1946 she visited the sacred grove "in a canoe, a fortnight earlier than the stipulated date and the sea was too rough for the figures to be observed." But by then she had come to speculate on a possible connection with the Esiẹ figures:

The description of the figures given to me by the priest made me wonder whether they are connected perhaps with the stone figures in the sacred grove at Esiẹ . . . These figures, as evidence shows, were dumped there by a people in flight — possibly the Asebu, who, when they were driven out of the Benin area strayed first into the Ife region and the area to the north of it . . .

Although any connection between the Asebu and the Esiẹ images appears tenuous at best, more detailed investigations in this area of Ghana might prove interesting.[4]

Esiẹ and Other West African Artistic Traditions

Whereas the Asebu figures remain legend, comparisons have been suggested between the Esiẹ stones and known art styles elsewhere. It has been generally acknowledged that the Esiẹ figures bear little affinity to any known traditions of sculpture in wood — but West African wood carving is highly perishable, and

so it cannot safely be concluded that the Esiẹ stones do not derive from a style previously established in wood. Indeed, both Fagg and Plass (1966:24) and Allison (1968:22) have suggested that a reason why so many of the figures have been decapitated is that their carvers were accustomed to working in wood; when the style of large and often extremely prognathic heads set on narrow necks was transposed to such a fragile medium as soapstone, the result was structurally unsound. In any case, this must remain conjecture; only sculpture in stone, terra-cotta, or metal, all extremely durable, offer reasonable bases for comparison.

Philip Allison's comprehensive survey of African stone sculpture (1968) discusses the various known traditions of stone carving, and for details the reader is referred to his writing. Although the majority of stone carvings have been executed in soapstone, a number of figures in basaltic or granitic rock have been found at various places. Of these, few sound bases for comparison with the Esiẹ stones can be found without stretching the imagination, although William Fagg (1959) has suggested an affinity between the treatment of the significantly aberrant Esiẹ head, H 546 (figs. V. 4-6) and the head of the famous "Idena" figure found in the Ore Grove in Ife (Murray and Willett 1958; Willett 1967:143; Allison 1968, Pl. 2; etc. The ear of this head is unlike any other at Esiẹ; it is unlike that of the Idena figure, too, but it does resemble some from the "post classical" period of Ifẹ; cf. Willett 1967).[5]

Donald Friend in 1939 reported the existence of fifteen small stone carvings in the Ekiti village of Efọn Alaaye. These were "little obelisks about a foot high, set in groups of three on small mounds. There are five such groups. The centre stone in one of these groups is carved as a human head with the tall cone-like coiffure that appears on Yoruban woodcarvings of women" (1939:108). These are of a granitic rock, and are currently housed in the Ifẹ Museum. Nowhere does Friend suggest any stylistic similarity between this group and the Esiẹ collection. His report is the second of a two-part study called "Stone Sculpture in Nigeria," and it follows that of Daniel (1939) on the Ofaro images which are of the Esiẹ style. Thus, Friend remarks that "the work is by no means as fine as that of Esiẹ," but he goes on to make some tantalizing suggestions:

. . . I feel sure that others exist in the neighbourhood that would well reward search . . . I was told by a native of Ikerre that some time ago — it cannot have been more than twenty years —

Chief Sapetu of that town had a number of stone figures of men and women with high head-dresses. They were kept in an Eshu [the Trickster deity[5]] shrine and sacrifices were made to them. They were smashed to pieces by ardent Christians so that today even fragments of them cannot be found.

Coincidences such as this, coupled with the Ekiti tribal marks on some of the Esie figures, should not be overlooked in the unravelling of the mystery of the origin of these sculptures.

So, as in the case of the "idols of Ikọle," we are left with another Mystery of the Lost Images. We are not told what Friend means by "Ekiti tribal marks." From one to three vertical pointed ellipsoid marks on each cheek are common on recent wood carvings from the area. Johnson (1921:108-9) describes and illustrates a uniquely Efọn pattern, a series of short parallel lines drawn horizontally and closely together to form "a dark patch on each cheek." Neither motif appears on any figure from Esiẹ. Some Ekiti sculpture displays one or two rows of raised dots or short slashes forming a herring-bone pattern between the eye and the ear; it may be these to which Friend is referring.

V.4. H 546, whose features suggest a possible Benin influence. This is one of six which were carved complete as heads: the others are H 128, H 244, H 245 (figs. V.20, 21), H 370, and H 545. Ht. 29 cm.

V.5. The right side of H 546.

V.6. The left side of H 546.

54

But any resemblance between these and the solid raised cicatrices behind the eyes of many of the Esie carvings is purely coincidental. The risks involved in using facial markings as a criterion for suggesting provenience will be discussed later. In any case, the Efon group has somehow come to be associated stylistically with Esie, so that in his discussion of the Esie stones Willett (1967:178) could remark, "Whatever their origin, they seem to have been traded fairly widely, for a number of small groups of figures in the same style have been found at Ofaro, Effon Alaye and Ijara, and recently in Ife itself." I have no pictures of the Efon stones, but I can simply and finally state that they bear no resemblance whatever to any figures from Esie.

An Ife Connection?

Willett's last reference is to a soapstone figure found in Modakeke, to which we shall presently return. But even in soapstone carving, comparisons with Esie can be made on only the most superficial — and hence very probably coincidental — of characteristics. Some bases for comparisions can be seen in the soapstone carvings of Ife — and, I must acknowledge, an Ife origin of the Esie stones cannot altogether be ruled out. William Fagg (1959:41) noted that Ife is "the only other known centre of stone sculpture for some hundreds of miles around." We have already noted the legend of the "four hundred and forty idols" of Ikole-Ekiti, alleged to have been taken there from Ife; a few versions of the Esie legends state that the "pale-skinned strangers" stopped at Ife before coming to Esie; and there is the tradition (cf. Chapter II, n. 3) that the original Elesie was the youngest son of Olofin — which would make him a brother of Akinsale, the first Elekole (the "Alakole" of Jones' account) of Ekiti! And Allison (1968:23) remarks the interesting fact that whereas the Igbomina of the savanna claim an Oyo origin, the first Orangun (ruler) of Ila, a large forest town only 15 miles south of Esie, whose inhabitants claim Igbomina affinity, was traditionally one of the seven grandsons of Odùduwà mentioned in an account of the original dispersion from Ife.

We should pause briefly at this point to consider such traditions of an Ife connection. Who the "seven grandsons of Odùduwà" were varies according to where the question is asked. In fact, like the "pieces of the True Cross," if all traditional rulers who claim descent from Odùduwà were polled, their numbers might well exceed seven times seven. Ife, in Yoruba tradition, was the site of the Creation, a place of primordial power, and the sanctions of kingship were first set down there by Odùduwà, himself having been commissioned by Olódùmárè, the Supreme Being (cf. Idowu 1962, and my own relation of the Ife myth, Stevens 1966). The authority of any traditional ruler, particularly in times of uncertain alliances, was naturally greatly enhanced if he could lay plausible claim to an ancestry of such lofty descent, seeking what Robin Law (1973) has called "the heritage of Oduduwa." Similarly, like the variant Esie legends, peoples who could claim to have passed through, if not to have resided in, Ife, during their migrations to their present sites, could thereby expect an unquestioned elevation of prestige. This is not to imply that any such claims were fradulent; rather, that they may accord with what I have elsewhere (Stevens 1975, 1978) argued is a very natural process of the selective alteration of historical tradition.

Philip Allison notes further that in the 19th-century wars with the Oyo of Ibadan, Ila-Orangun sided with Ekiti, Ilesa, and other forest states to the south (see Ajayi and Smith 1964:44-5). Allison brought to his ethnographic research a valuable background in forestry, and he has offered some ecological observations which raise some interesting questions about the history and identity of the Igbomina (see Chapter II, n. 1). Why the simultaneous claim to Igbomina *and* to Ife heritage by the peoples of Ila-Orangun and other southern towns, when their northern neighbours claim an Oyo origin? *If* we accept the southern groups' claim to Igbomina affinity, we can note, as Allison (1968:23) has, that the Igbomina as a whole effected both a savannah and a forest adaptation. We can therefore logically surmise that, in this process of adaptation, the southern groups were increasingly isolated from their northern counterparts, not only by the forest, but also by the mountainous terrain which characterizes the High Forest zone. The claim to an Ife heritage by those in the south could then possibly be explained by the processes of the political distortion of tradition to which I have briefly referred, above. But on the other hand, it could be argued, the same process of distortion might possibly account for the northern, savannah Igbomina claim to an Old Oyo origin!

Furthermore, Allison earlier (1964:105,n.1) had observed that Yoruba stone carving is found almost exclusively in forested country, and in areas of Derived Savannah, in which human expansion has pushed the edge of the forest southward; such areas include Esiẹ, Ijara, and Ofaro. This is an interesting correlation, but we have no evidence to consider it a causal one.

To return to stylistic affinities with the art of Ifẹ, Allison (1968:23-4) continues:

> Tradition associates the images with a forest people within the cultural sphere of Ifẹ, whose influence can be detected in several recurrent features of the carvings. The elaborate headdresses, overall facial markings, waistcloths tied with a sash, long multi-stringed necklaces and cotton-reel stools, all appear in the art of Ifẹ. Compared with any surviving examples of Yoruba wood-carving the style of the stone figures is less conventionalized and more characterized, but might well represent a stage in the development from the classical naturalism of Ifẹ to the formalism of recent carvings in wood.

He acknowledges that "the steatite carvings to be seen on the shrines of Ifẹ today have nothing in common with those of Esiẹ," but adds, "a single example showing some affinities with the Esiẹ style has recently been found at Ifẹ."

The figure to which Willett and Allison have referred is here illustrated for the first time (figs. V. 7, 8). It was found in 1961 in Modakẹkẹ, a village bordering Ifẹ, at a depth of approximately 62 cm. while digging the foundations for a house. It is a standing figure of a male, 31 cm. high, unfortunately headless. According to Professor Willett (personal communication, 1975), an affinity to the Esiẹ style was suggested on the bases of 1) the arms are carved free of the body, 2) it wears a skirt tied with a sash, and 3) its spine is represented by an incised line. These are, in fact, features represented in many of the Esiẹ stones. But similarities stop there. The treatment of the nipples and navel, and the hands clasped over the belly, are features that set it quite apart from anything at Esiẹ. The pendant on the chest also has no Esiẹ parallel. There are, we should note, eight standing figures at Esiẹ (HT 195, 200, 279; T 136, 139, 183, 198, 790), but none shows any marked similarity to this piece. I would suggest, rather, that the features of the Modakẹkẹ image mark a

V.7. Soapstone figure found in Modakẹkẹ, Ifẹ, in 1961 during excavations for the foundations of a house. Ht. 31 cm.

V.8. Rear view of the Modakẹkẹ image.

unique Ifẹ style of soapstone carving, and for comparison I submit a photograph of the soapstone carvings of Ọbàtálá, the Creator God (known also as Òrìṣà Nlá, the Great Òrìṣà), and Yemọo, his wife and the goddess of certain watery places (fig. V. 9).[7] I took this photograph in 1965, inside the house of the former holder of the title of Chief Ọbalale, the chief priest of the cult of Òrìṣà Nlá, at Ideta-Ile, in the Itapa quarter of Ifẹ. The only other published views of these images are Pierre Verger's flash-assisted picture taken in the inner room of the shrine of Òrìṣà Nlá (1954:pl. 73), and my shots of them painted for the annual festival (Stevens 1966:191-3).

Both have hands clasped across the belly. The arms of Yemọo are fused with the body, but those of Ọbàtálá are clear from elbow to shoulder. The nipples of the Ọbàtálá figure, and the navels of both, are similar to those of the Modakẹkẹ image. The skirts of leaves strung together are periodically replaced with fresh ones, and it strikes me that the decoration of the skirt of the Modakẹkẹ figure does not represent stripes, as the Ifẹ Museum catalogue entry describes it, but rather leaves such as these. The face of Ọbàtálá

is heavily striated, much in the manner of some of the Esiẹ pieces, but also in a style similar to many others of Ifẹ.

I have been decrying the use of comparisons as conclusive data, but I cannot resist showing a picture (fig. V. 10) of the dwarf-like standing bronze figure at Tada,[8] a Nupe village on the Niger near Jebba, to suggest that this, from overall treatment down to the nipples and navel, shows far greater similarity to the Modakẹkẹ image than does any figure at Esiẹ.

The "several recurrent features" in the Esiẹ collection which Allison suggests show an Ifẹ "influence" are general characteristics which have many counterparts elsewhere. There are, however, a few specific elements which do have parallels in Ifẹ art and culture. Willett (1967:178) has noted two carvings representing calabashes of the type customarily used for palm wine, a motif found in Ifẹ art. There are, in fact, three. Two are free-standing, apparently never part of a group; these are pictured in the Plates section, under the heading, "Miscellaneous Objects." The third is part of a group, and I picture it here (figs. V. 11, 12) as well as with the Plates, for it combines

V.9. The images of Yemọo (l.) and Ọbàtálá, in the house of the priest of Orisa Nla, Ideta-ile, Ifẹ. Hts. approx. 53 cm.

V.10. A bronze figure at Tada, one of the so-called "Tsoede Bronzes." Compare this with the Modakẹkẹ image, figs. V.7, 8. Photographed in 1965. Ht. approx. 50 cm.

57

some other interesting elements as well. This is a kneeling figure of a woman (HT 270, 55 cm. in height), firmly holding a calabash between her legs. She is one of eleven kneeling figures, the others being HT 273, 274, 275, 276, and T 15, 181, 317, 324, 532, 801.

Of the kneeling figures, eight are naked, and these, with T 476 which is seated, are the only naked figures in the entire collection. HT 270 alone is dressed, in the typical waistcloth. Only one, HT 275, is obviously male; the sex of HT 276 cannot be determined. HT 273, T 15, T 317, and T 324 hold before them, in gestures of offering, what are most probably open pods of kola nuts. T 532 may also have held something; her arms converge toward the belly, but her hands are missing. T 181 has its arms crossed, palms flat on the breast, an apparent gesture of submission.

Nakedness, femininity, a kneeling posture, a gesture of offering — all signify servility. Domestic servants are often children, or adolescents. HT 273 and HT 275 are most probably children, and some of the others may be, too — with the obvious exception of T 801, who is clearly pregnant. Are these slaves, servants, or attendants upon a royal household? According to the people of Esiẹ, the kneeling figures were the attendants to the King, and they were all arranged near him in the old House of Images, as were the two individual calabashes. Ht 270 (dressed, most certainly adult) is regarded as the King's Chief Attendant, and she was selected (with HT 273, stolen in 1974) to attend the King on his new altar (see fig. I. 26).

Kings everywhere have their servants and concubines. But what is significant about these servile figures to our present discussion is that two of the six complete images, HT 270 and HT 273, display half-shaven heads. (The hairstyles of HT 274 and HT 276 have been obliterated.) This motif is found on two other figures as well, the seated HT 271, and the fragmentary HT 272. Contrary to Daniel's (1937:46) suggestion, these probably do not represent àbíkú disfigurations. Àbíkú, meaning "we are born to die," is a class of spirits of children who are forever trying to lure other children to join them; this partially accounts for infant mortality. If a mother has lost a child to the àbíkú, she may give her next child an àbíkú name, containing an entreaty to the spirits not to take this one. If several children have been lost in this way, subsequent infants may be mildly disfigured to make them less attractive to the spirits. Such disfigurement may include shaving part of the head, or, as Johnson (1921:84) describes, shaving all but a circular topknot, as seen in the figure of the boy, HT

V.11. HT 270, one of the "attendants" to the King of the Images. She holds what is probably a calabash for palm-wine. Her half-shaved head suggests she was designated as one of the Ìlárí, the royal servants and messengers. She is one of many images who are obviously victims of willful damage; her face and breasts have been slashed off. Ht. 55 cm.

V.12. Side view of HT 270. Although it is not easily visible, she wears a skirt, which extends a bit below mid-thigh.

V.13. T 458. An Ifẹ influence is indicated in the looped stool; this is the only such stool in the collection. But the loop is quite unlike those on some of the stools of classical Ifẹ, suggesting that the artist fashioned his version from vaguely-reported information. The base of the stool is missing; it extended downward from the centre column. Ht. 34.5 cm.

275. But this practice is discontinued as the child matures and seems likely to survive, hence it could not account for the half-shaven head of HT 270, the adult wine-bearer. These servile figures with half-shaven heads, rather, could only represent the Ìlàrí, male and female servants to the King (see Abraham 1958:19-20). The males are messengers and body-guards; each has a female counterpart whom he addresses as Ìyá, Mother. The Oni of Ifẹ has his Ìlàrí even today, but as Akinjogbin (1967:118 and 1971:335) has pointed out, Ìlàrí were found in the courts of many Yoruba ọbas; in fact, the institution originated in Ọyọ. We shall return to this shortly.

Both Allison and Willett have seen counterparts in Ifẹ art to the type of stools most of the Esiẹ images sit upon. The prominent stool type of Ifẹ, however, had a loop of uncertain purpose, extending outward from the center of the column and curving back just under the seat (cf. Fagg and Fagg 1960). Apparently, as illustrated in the large terra-cotta from the Iwinrin Grove (Willett 1967: pl. 76), this large loop extended over a smaller rectangular stool on which the seated

person rested his feet. Willett (1967:177) notes that in basic design the Esiẹ stools resemble those of Ifẹ, but they lack this loop. To add one final bit of supportive evidence for those who seek an Ifẹ connection, or agree with Allison that the Esiẹ stones might represent a post-classical Ifẹ stage, I include here a photograph (fig. V. 13) of T 458, which sits upon a looped stool. The loop, however, extends to the rear and does not project beyond the seat. As I shall suggest later, this figure most likely was inspired by Ifẹ, but was not produced there.

Similarities Elsewhere

We are obliged to consider all the above, but we can also find similarities in art styles elsewhere. Most writers have been struck by the elaborate coiffures on many of the images. One particular style, seen in HT 259, 260, 261, H 331 through 360, and in the reconstructed H348-T 95 (fig. V.1), resembles nothing found at Ife' but is identical to that of some of the terra-cottas comprising the so-called "Nok culture," found at various sites to the west and south of the escarpment of the Jos Plateau. Most striking is the hairstyle of the life-size head (B. Fagg 1956) currently on display in the National Museum, Lagos. To this I add the previously unpublished photograph (fig. V. 14) of the upper half of a head, slightly smaller than life-size, found in a tin mine at Jemaa, currently in the Jos Museum. A similar hairstyle, still practiced by women of the Fulani and other northern peoples, is effected by braiding the ends of a large tuft of hair around a string; the string is then pulled out and the hair puffs up in bouffant fashion.

Fagg and Plass (1964:8-9), Willett (1967:114), and others have observed that predominant basic forms in Nok art are the cylinder and the cone. The heads of Nok sculptures, Willett notes, are often cylindrical or cone-shaped, set at an angle upon another cylinder forming the neck and body. He compares this construction with that of the soapstone *nomoli* figures of the Sherbro of Sierra Leone (and Allison, 1968:36ff., notes that similar observations can be made of the *pomtan* of the Kissi of Guinea), and with a group of the Esiẹ figures. Structurally the comparison is interesting, but most probably coincidental; in any case, there exists no ethnographic nor historic justification for such a comparison. The drawing of an Esiẹ figure Willett illustrates (1967: 114) is of HT 92 (fig. V. 15);

with this we can compare HT 237 (fig. V. 16). The "group" he mentions which "has a structure of the head and neck which is very similar to that of many of the Nok sculptures" p. 117) could comprise a great many of the figures, particularly the strikingly prognathic ones, most of which have been decapitated (cf. such "groups" as H 49-63, 73-78, 139, 140, 162-171, 202-4, etc.). Willett notes further that "the form of the ear echoes some of the Nok and modern Yoruba pieces."

The best radiocarbon dates for Nok thus far established indicate that it spans a period at least as long as from the middle of the first millennium B.C. to later than the second century A.D. It cannot, of course, be contended that the Esiẹ figures are as old. But Willett (1967:117) observes that:

> so many features of the Nok culture, particularly of its art, are found in later cultures elsewhere in West Africa, that it is difficult not to believe that the Nok culture as we know it represents the ancestral stock from which much of the sculptural tradition of West Africa derives.

This is certainly possible, and until archaeology unearths other culture complexes, we must go on what we have.

Comparisons between Esiẹ and sculptural traditions elsewhere could be pursued still further. Willett (1967:177-8, and pls. 102-4), for example, sees a resemblance between the facial marks on some of the figures and those of some of the bronzes from Igbo-Ukwu (cf. Shaw 1970). We could point out, too, that similar marks, particularly forehead striations like those on the image of Ọbàtálá (fig. V. 9), appear on several of the terra-cottas excavated recently near Ifẹ by O. Eluyẹmi of the Ifẹ University Institute of African Studies.

Milburn (quoted by Daniel, 1937:48) notes that in some of the images, "the ear is carved at the back of the head instead of at the top end of the jaw. This convention is to be seen in the wooden figure at the entrance to the house of the Ọrangun of Ila [now in the entrance hall of the Nigerian Museum, Lagos⁹]. It is found in company with an extremely long and prognathous jaw." Esiẹ heads in this style are many; see, for example, H 49-63, 73-78, 162-172, and others

V.14. The upper half of a terra-cotta head of the "Nok Culture", found in a tin mine at Jemaa. Slightly smaller than life-size.

discussed earlier (p. 60) as showing a structural affinity to Nok sculpture. But Milburn adds that "wood carvings with these features are to be seen in many places;" indeed, this is quite a common feature in recent Yoruba wood carving.

Frobenius (Chapter I, pp. 1-2) has seen a similarity between Esię coiffures and those of some Benin bronzes of the "Dutch period," the mid-seventeenth century, and Meyerowitz (1943:32) finds echoes of the Benin "court costume" in the jewellery and dress of the entire collection. So let me add that in the treatment of the eyes, nostrils, and lips of the aberrant head (H 546, figs. V. 4-6) which William Fagg has likened to the Idena figure of Ifę, I see rather a Benin affinity.

And so, in the Esię collection we can see something akin to elements in most of the great West African artistic traditions, but to none of them can we find affinities strong enough to suggest origins. This need not be a problem, however; as I will suggest later, the great diversity of possible "influences" may in itself provide us with a clue as to the area of origin of the Esię stones.

V.15. HT 92, showing a typical treatment of the head and neck which has been seen as similar to some Nok sculpture, as well as some *nomoli* figures of the Sherbro of Sierra Leone, and some *pomtan* figures of the Kissi of Guinea. Compare HT 237, fig. V.16. Ht. 44 cm.

Inferences from Contemporary Ethnography: Facial Marks

Various aspects of dress, accoutrements including jewellery, weapons, and tools, stool design, and body and facial scarification seen in the Esię images have many parallels in the "material culture" of contemporary populations, and it can be tempting to draw inferences about their origins on the bases of such comparisons, But here again, such inferences are inconclusive at best, possibly misleading at worst. If, for example, societal parallels were drawn on the basis of the possession of this or that trait, possible sources of diffusion could be found among Western Ibo, Igbirra, Jarawa, Tera, Nupe, Hausa-Fulani, Bariba, and various Yoruba groups, to mention a few.

Much has been made of the "tribal" facial markings on many of the images. The most common marks are three raised parallel lines, each about 3 cm. long, about mid-way between the eye and the ear. In some instances these extend from the corner of the eye to the ear. Most early writers have designated these,

V.16. HT 237. Compare HT 92, fig. V.15. Ht. 51 cm.

allegedly on the basis of the local peoples' perception, as Nupe. But Oyinloye (1953), I think rightly, states

> The figures with three parallel and horizontal marks at the back of the eye do not represent the Nupes as supposed. The Nupes have their three marks in a triangular form near the mouth. My investigations indicate that the tribal marks of the Esie figures are Yoruba, though their use was long ago abandoned.

Indeed, the suggestion of a Nupe origin of these marks is puzzling. The idea certainly did not originate with the people of Esie as Milburn (quoted by Daniel, 1937:48), Meyerowitz (1943:35), and others have alleged. During 1965 and 1966 I interviewed a great many elders, including the Àwòrò, regarding their perceptions of the images, and the only figure they pointed out as being Nupe is HT 58, which the people call *"Tapa"* (the Yoruba word for Nupe), whose head is pictured in fig V. 17. That this is by far the largest image (110 cm., weighing 104 kg.) might suggest a significant Nupe influence; but this is the *only* figure consistently held by my informants to be Nupe. Three pairs of parallel lines beginning just beneath the lower lip and running over the chin, the central pair

V.17. Head of HT 58, called *"Tapa"* (Nupe) by Esie people. The marks on the chin are used by some modern Nupe; but there is no record of the use of the parallel lines back of the eye, among Nupe. Similar marks appear on H 131 (see Plates).

straight, the other two curving away, are marks seen on Nupe of today and recent times. Identical marks are seen on H 131. Strictly speaking, however, none of the images exhibits *traditional* Nupe marks. According to S. F. Nadel, whose *A Black Byzantium* is still the most complete ethnography of the Nupe, there are "no tribal costume, or tribal emblems . . . no tattoos or face-markings characteristic of all Nupe" (1942:14); rather, like the Yoruba, the kingdom was comprised of a number of semi-autonomous subtribes, each designated by a unique set of marks. The traditional feature common to most was a single heavy line running from the side of the nose down and outward across each cheek (1942:405-6). No Esie image displays such marks. The traditional Nupe marks most closely resembling those on some images at Esie are the three vertical lines on the chin, used by the central Beni (the people of Bida, the modern Nupe capital, and its environs); but among the Esie images these are almost invariably accompanied by the three eye-ear marks, and often by corresponding raised vertical cicatrices at the back of the neck.

The "modern" marks of the Beni and a few other subtribes, e.g. the Nupe Zam, Kusopa, Ebagi, and Kakanda, are the three "cat's whiskers" at the corners of the mouth, referred to by Oyinloye, similar to marks found on some Ife and Benin sculpture (but on none of the Esie stones). Indeed, these may have been of Yoruba origin. They were used by the Yagba (Johnson 1921:105, 109), the most north-easterly Yoruba group, situated between the Igbomina and the Kakanda. A Nupe occupational grouping, called generically *Konu*, the principal weavers and dyers, are descended from Yagba, brought to Nupe land as slaves (Nadel 1942:20; Forde 1955:20). Nadel offers some observations on this possibility — and on the ever-changing nature and distribution of facial markings:

> Fashion is changing the markings to-day — and there is no reason to assume that this has not always been so. I have seen fathers and sons whose faces bore different markings. The markings of the Bida people, like other fashions associated with the capital of the kingdom, have been adopted by the people of the districts. And the modern Beni and Bida markings are in turn said to have been adopted originally from the Yoruba, whose less conspicuous facial marks the Nupe found "nicer" than their own crude slashes (1942:22, n. 1).

Facial marks diffuse and change readily and rapidly; they are not the exclusive property of a distinct group, preserved as that group's badge of identity since time immemorial. They are, therefore, unreliable for ascribing origins of art objects. Willett (1967:pl. 93) notes that the cat's whiskers marks occur in sculpture of Benin and Ifẹ, but that similar marks are found also among the Igala, the Jukun (from whom both the Kakanda and the Yagba are allegedly derived; Elphinstone 1921:48), and even the Senufo of the Ivory Coast, all of whom have well-established artistic traditions. Parallels to the several Esiẹ heads with full facial scarification are found frequently in Ifẹ art, but the practice is today most commonly found among some northern groups, such as Gwari, Jarawa, Tera, and others. Willett (1976:pl. 34) pictures a Tera man bearing such marks. I have seen such marks on persons in Maiduguri, in parts of Adamawa and Sardauna Provinces, and on persons from the northern Cameroons — but I also found an Ibadan taxi-driver bearing a crude representation of some of the Esiẹ marks on his right cheek (fig. V. 18). His left cheek bore a different pattern; eight short horizontal marks in sets of four, a pattern identified by Johnson (1921:104) as a variant of the àbàjà (called by him ẹsẹ, lit. "rows of things"), traditionally a typical Ọyọ mark. The man, one Alabede, could offer no suggestion as to the significance of his marks, but he confirmed that both his mother and father were of Ibadan lineages. Ibadan was settled by Ọyọ refugees.

Esiẹ people told me that the unusual raised spirals (or concentric circles — it is difficult to tell which was intended) on the cheeks of three severed heads, H 255 (fig. V.19), H 284, and H 310, are Bariba marks. I did not visit Borgu, and was unable otherwise to confirm this report. Temple and Temple (1919:76), however, describe the Bariba mark as "a broad line extending for about three inches from the bridge of the nose downwards, on one or both sides of the face." Similar circular marks appear on the cheeks of some Ifẹ terra-cottas, however (cf. Willett 1967:pl. 14).

One unusual head, H 245 (figs. V. 20, 21), has four deep incised lines from eye to ear and, almost as an afterthought, three fine straight lines from the corner of the mouth nearly to the ear. I know of no ethnographic parallels. It may be significant that this head is one of six (including H 546,[10] figs. V. 4-6) which were indisputably complete as heads. The others are H 128, 244, 370, and 545. All of these are in some sense aberrant, showing few of the general characteristics common to most of the other stones. H 245, as well as H 128 and H 244, seem closer in style to the terra-cotta head, TC 1 (figs. IV. 1, 2); H 545 resembles more closely the terra-cotta head fragment, TC 2 (fig. IV. 3), than it does any of the stone figures.

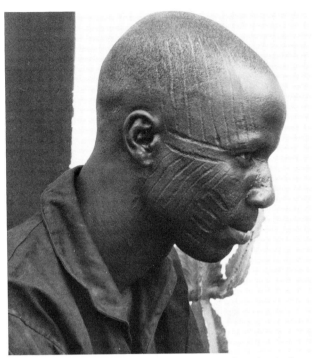

V.18. Alabede, an Ibadan taxi-driver, with facial marks similar to those on some of the Esiẹ stones. He affirmed that both his parents were of Ibadan lineages. Photographed in 1966. Facial marks diffuse widely and rapidly, and are unreliable indicators of the provenience of art objects that are more than a few generations old.

V.19. H 255. The concentric circles on the cheek have been reported for Bariba, but similar marks are found on some classical Ifẹ terra-cottas. Compare H 284 and H 310 (Plates). Ht. 24 cm.

No parallels whatsoever have been found to the three raised vertical cicatrices on the napes of a great number of the images, which Daniel (1937:47) reports "are said to be in common use at the present time, and to represent incisions made for the insertion of magical protective medicines."

Many of the images show elaborate body scarification as well. I will make no attempt to find contemporary ethnographic parallels for these; some representative patterns are shown in detail in the Plates.

Under the heading of "scarification" we might consider other examples of physical mutilation, such as the filing of upper incisor teeth to points, seen in H 131 and H 143 (Plates section). Such a practice has been reported from various parts of West Africa from time to time, particularly in the savannah areas. I have seen cases of it among Dakakari of Kontagora Province.

And finally, and perhaps most frustratingly, *none* of the images bears the traditional Igbomina marks, three horizontal parallel lines at the center of the cheek (Johnson 1921:105, 109).

Other Features

The origins and diffusion patterns of facial marks are elusive, and attempting to trace the geographical distribution of any of the marks on the Esiẹ stones is difficult at best; inconclusive where successful. Parallels from contemporary populations can easily be found for most of the other accoutrements on the Esiẹ figures; again, however, such parallels are inconclusive. In aspects of dress Meyerowitz (1943:32) sees a Benin affinity:

> On the whole their costume is reminiscent of the court costume worn, to this day, by the Benin aristocracy, consisting of a full long skirt, rows of necklaces of different length, made usually of the red Ilorin stone bead, and bracelets of different types.

Several Yoruba, and Hausa, traits have been recognized in aspects of dress and jewellry by Daniel (1937:47). Esiẹ people supplied me with terms for types of jewellery which they recognized as typically Yoruba; such specifics, where applicable, are indicated in the captions to the Plates.

Among the most striking aspects of the collection is that the great majority of the figures are seated on

V.20. H 245, one of the six heads complete as heads (see fig. V.5). The overall treatment may be compared more profitably to the terra-cotta head, TC 1 (figs. IV.1, 2), than to any of the other stone figures. The head was designed to lie flat, on a shelf or altar. The angle at which its flat back was cut (see fig. V.21) ensures that it lies slightly propped up, so that the face looks forward. Ht. 22 cm.

V.21. H 245, side.

stools of a type comprised of a circular seat supported by a cylindrical shaft rising from a circular base. The exceptions are the eleven kneeling figures already discussed (pp. 58-59), the eight standing figures (HT 195, 200, 279; T 136, 139, 183, 198, 790) and nine figures seated on rectangular, sometimes anvil-shaped benches (HT 124; T 58, 67, 80, 94, 96, 439, 703, 745). The shafts of the mushroom-shaped stools are sometimes decorated in grooved, spiral, diamond, or other motifs; identical stools are in use among the Igbirra. Fig. V. 22 shows some examples, photographed in a village north of Okene.

Some items of musical instruments, tools, weaponry, and other trappings are interesting and so carefully executed as to give the impression that they must have had specific cultural models. Many of them, particularly the ornate daggers and cutlasses, have Northern counterparts. That a military (and possibly hunting) element predominates, there seems little doubt. Extreme care was taken in the delineation of weapons—in a few cases, even bow *strings* were carved (see "Miscellaneous Objects," in the Plates section). Milburn (in Daniel 1937:48) remarks on the absence of any equestrian figures, whereas the mounted warrior is a motif common in Yoruba wood-carving — but we must hesitate to draw firm conclusions from this observation. But a preoccupation with the militaristic attitude of so many of the figures — particularly the females — has raised some speculation to which we must address ourselves.

One figure, HT 79 (fig. V. 23) has a curious narrow cross-hatching extending from the temples to the chin. Oyinloye (1953) states that it represents an "iron mask." This could be construed to represent chain-mail. A.D.H. Bivar (1964) discusses some of the many protective garments of mail, probably all imported, which were in use in some northern areas from the late fifteenth century up to recent times. Examples of mail shirts and coats are on view in the Jos and Kano museums. I have found no record of facial armour having been used in the southern Sudan, however. Robert Smith (1967) discusses styles of Yoruba arms, but makes no mention of mail having ever been worn, either by foot-soldiers or cavalry; he mentions only that Yoruba warriors wore "many pocketed and padded war jackets of a type still used by Yoruba hunters" (p. 101). And, if the pattern on the cheeks of HT 79 represents armour, why does the figure lack any other military trappings? Another such head was photographed in the early 1950's by K. C. Murray; this is now missing from the collection and the accom-

panying photograph (fig. V. 24), poor as it is, is the only one available. The cross-hatch pattern on this head covers the forehead, temples, cheeks, and upper lip as well as the chin. Facial and body hair is customarily represented in West African sculpture by cross-hatching. Indeed several of the Esie heads display cross-hatching at the hair line, and pubic hair is so designated in T 476. We can only conclude that the similar patterns on HT 79 and on the Murray head represent full beards.

One further line of thinking based on a militaristic element has encouraged some to seek the origins of the Esie stones outside the political boundaries of modern Nigeria. In West African sculpture, determining the intended sex of a figure is sometimes difficult. Where they are exposed, the genitals are certain indicators; but the breasts are sometimes equally pronounced in both sexes. Hairstyles, jewellry, and dress do not appear to correlate sexually in the Esie collection. Such correlations *might* appear when a statistical analysis has been completed, but for the present I have relied on breast accentuation. Some of the figures are too abraded or fragmentary to make a positive determination, but where the breasts are clearly more than mere nubs, I have designated a figure as female.

Based on this criterion, fully one-third of the figures are female, and of these about a quarter are armed, as if for war. Of the total number of such militaristic figures, an interesting correlation does appear: the men are archers and wielders of daggers; the women carry cutlasses. In fact, no figure that is positively female (T 35 is questionable) wears a quiver; only a few of the males hold cutlasses. The great majority of the female cutlass-bearers hold their weapons in the right hand, the point resting on the right shoulder (the only apparent exception is T 1, who holds what appears to be a cutlass in her left hand).

These militaristic females, the majority with raised cutlasses (a few hold their weapons point-down, some have them resting across their laps) may well represent important personages. Milburn (in Daniel 1937:49) noted that the figures "seem to come from a people whose women were respected and could hold positions of authority." But earlier (p. 48) he had asked a rhetorical question which has prompted some speculation that the origin of the Esie images might lie not only outside Yorubaland, but beyond the modern political boundaries of Nigeria: "can the women with swords be related to the Amazons of Dahomey?"

65

V.22. Carved wooden stools in use among Igbirra, photographed in a village north of Okene in 1965. The height of the stool at lower left is 30 cm.

The Armed Females: A Dahomean Connection?

Much has been written about these redoutable female warriors, who were unique in Africa. Exaggeration has not been necessary in describing their organization and their near-suicidal ferocity in combat. They were known officially as *ahosi*, "the King's wives," although in the proper sense of the word they were wives to no one. During their military service they were quartered apart and were expected to remain totally celibate under penalty of death to both offending parties. In their ceremonial praise-chants they spoke of themselves as no longer women, but men; and they appear to have been selected for their strength and stamina from among the potential sexual partners whom the King had rejected as being unattractive, and whose appearance and behaviour ran counter to Dahomean ideals of femininity. But they were held in extreme respect; general esteem for them, as well as recognition of their inaccessibility as sexual partners, is conveyed in the term by which, according to Burton, they were popularly known: *meno*, "our mothers."

Their reported numbers vary according to different accounts, but they seem at any one time to have comprised between 4000 and 6000 of the total armed forces. Their recruitment, disciplined military regimen, weaponry, organization, tactics and conduct in the field, are described by 18th-century visitors to the kingdom, including Captain William Snelgrave (1734), Robert Norris (1789:94), and Archibald Dalzel (1793:55); these assessments are corroborated by such 19th-century accounts as Forbes (1851,ii:89-91), Skertchly (1874:454-5), and Burton (1864, ii:42ff). These and other accounts are recounted by Herskovits (1938, ii). The "Amazons" are seen as responsible for several important military victories, most notably the rout of Whydah in 1727. T. J. Bowen (1857:118-20) recorded his eye-witness account of the Battle of Abeokuta in March 1851, in which a Dahomean force of 16,000, including 6000 Amazons, engaged the Egba in a long and bloody battle. Although they were finally repulsed, the Dahomeans forcefully impressed upon their opponents the ferocity of their women warriors (Ajayi and Smith 1964:37-9).

Could these women have been the models for the armed females of Esiẹ? Or, further, could the Esiẹ collection be of Dahomean origin? Several scholars, most recently Akinjogbin (1971:305-343) have reconstructed the long history of a close, albeit not always friendly, relationship between Dahomey and the Yoruba kingdom of Ọyọ. Ọyọ invaded Dahomey a

V.23. HT 79. The narrow cross-hatched band from the temple to the chin is most probably a beard, and not facial armour, as has previously been supposed. Ht. 61 cm.

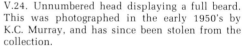

V.24. Unnumbered head displaying a full beard. This was photographed in the early 1950's by K.C. Murray, and has since been stolen from the collection.

number of times in the early 18th century, and perhaps earlier. In 1730 a treaty was agreed upon, which was subsequently broken; but in 1748 the Dahomean king Tegbesu concluded a treaty which remained unbroken until the 1830's. Tegbesu had spent ten years as a voluntary hostage in Ọyọ, and he had become quite familiar with and congenial toward its people and their customs. Indeed, his familiarity with and rapport with this powerful and ever threatening neighbour may well have been a factor in his accession to the throne (Akinjogbin 1971:111). Tegbesu consolidated his reign and encouraged intercourse with Ọyọ. A great amount of cultural exchange took place and, Akinjogbin (1971:334) notes, until the end of the 18th century Dahomey and Ọyọ could properly be regarded as "two parts of the same empire." To aid in his efforts to centralise authority in Dahomey, Tegbesu adopted a number of Ọyọ customs and institutions, among them the Ìlàrí system (which we have discussed earlier, p. 59):

> The Ilari were the people whom the Europeans called 'half heads' from the way their hair was cut. They were, throughout the Yoruba country, messengers-cum-civil-servants used by certain classes of Oba (Kings). The advantage of this class of people for Tegbesu was that they were mobile, could be sent to any part of the Kingdom and thus used to check any remote officer or coordinate any national plans. From 1745 onwards, the Ilari were frequently sent down to the Europeans' forts (Akinjogbin 1967:118).

Akinjogbin concludes that, while students of Dahomean history have tended to emphasize the oppressive aspects of that kingdom's subservience to Ọyọ throughout most of the 18th century, the 60-odd years of peace allowed Tegbesu to consolidate his government and to shore up — at least temporarily — the shaky Dahomean economy. "Without the administrative machinery, particularly the Ìlàrí system, copied from Ọyọ by Tegbesu, the government of the enlarged kingdom of Dahomey would undoubtedly have been much less efficient" (1967:211). We know little of other aspects of the "cultural exchange" that took place between these two kingdoms. We do not know what use, if any, Tegbesu might have made of the "Amazons" during this period.[11] Frustratingly absent in the histories is a discussion of either Dahomean or Ọyọ sculptural traditions. And there is no mention of what sort of booty the invading Ọyọ armies might have taken as a result of their several raids early in the century. But if we accept what seems to have been a general assumption, that there was no significant female presence in Yoruba armies, hence the models for the armed females of Esiẹ must be foreign, then it seems plausible to make one of two deductions: 1) The Esiẹ images are Dahomean in origin, and found their way into Yorubaland some time during the 18th century. The presence of the four Ìlàrí figures, and others showing what seem to be distinctly Yoruba traits, could be explained in this way also. 2) The period of peace resultant from Tegbesu's treaty could have allowed for a rise in artistic productivity in Ọyọ, and that Ọyọ, or other Yoruba sculptors, well aware of the reputation of the Amazons, could have used them as models for the armed females. The subservience of Dahomey to Ọyọ could be indicated in the attitudes of these figures, many of whom hold their cutlasses raised in what might be attitudes of salute. Pursuing this idea, we can imagine that the Esiẹ collection represents the court of Ọyọ and representatives of its subject peoples. This latter suggestion is, in fact, an attractive possibility, and we shall re-examine it later.

But there seem at least two persuasive arguments *against* deducing a Dahomean origin of, or inspiration for, the Esiẹ images, based on reference to the Amazons.

First, the best historical evidence available places the earliest use of female warriors during the reign of Agaja (1708-c.1730), Tegbesu's predecessor. Agaja had conquered the coastal areas, notably Whydah and Popo, but then had suffered a debilitating invasion by Ọyọ. The coastal states saw their opportunity and regained their former territories. Captain Snelgrave (1734:125-7), quoted by Herskovits (1938,ii:84-5) who was personally familiar with Agaja, records how, in 1727, the king resolved his "State of Perplexity:"

> when he had not a sufficient number of Soldiers to encounter the Whidaws and Popoes together, and on the other hand, could not bear to see himself braved by such a cowardly race as the Whidaws, his Policy extricated him out of this Difficulty. He ordered a great Number of Women to be armed like Soldiers, and appointed Officers to each Company, with Colours, Drums and Umbrellas . . . Then ordering the Army to march, the Women Soldiers were placed in the Rear, to prevent Discovery. When they came in sight of the Whidaw Army, the latter were much surprized to see such Numbers of Dahome Soldiers, as they supposed them all to be, marching against them; For they had much depended on the former Reports, that they were so far reduced, as not to be able (at least so soon) to have made

Head against them. At this unexpected sight the *Whidaws* were divided . . .

There seems, in fact, little doubt that Agaja was the first to employ women as warriors; had they been used earlier their reputation would surely have been widespread, and it would have been unlikely that Agaja could have thus surprised the Whydah army. Tegbesu apparently had little use for the Amazons, although he posted armed women as guards (Norris 1789:94). By the middle of the 19th century the *ahosi* ("king's wives," as the female warriors were known) had become a firmly established institution, utilized most effectively by King Gezo in the Battle of Abeokuta, 1851. But there is no evidence that women were used in military operations prior to 1727 and, as I hope to suggest more persuasively later, the Esìẹ stones were most probably carved well before that date. Moreover, we know that the institution of the `Ilárí was introduced into Dahomey by Tegbesu; if a Dahomean origin of the Esìẹ stones were sought, the presence of `Ìlàrí figures in the collection would place their manufacture toward the middle of the 18th century.

Second, Snelgrave reports that Agaja's female warriors were "armed like Soldiers." The most effective of the Dahomean troops were, by that time, armed with muskets (Herskovits 1938,ii:73-74; Snelgrave 1734:77-9). As the institution of the *ahosi* developed, it seems that *all* female combat troops were equipped with muskets; some carried cutlasses as well. But firearms are not represented in the Esìẹ collection.

A final, and least conclusive, observation is that the "Amazons," from the time of their inception, seem to have been dressed in tunics and caps, like their male counterparts. All of the Esìẹ images are naked above the waist.

The Ìyálôde

Arguments for a Dahomean origin of the Esìẹ images, making reference to the armed females, have been based on the assumption that there were no women in positions of authority in Yoruba military organization. This, however, is a false assumption.

Eva Meyerowitz, discussing the images in 1943, had called attention to a significant Yoruba political institution:

> . . . a surprising feature is the women carrying

curved swords or cutlasses, reminding us that women wielded great political power at the courts of ancient African kingdoms; we only need to think of the Iyalode, the 'queens of the ladies' representing the women at the courts of the Yoruba kings, who had their lieutenants like all other principal chiefs and commanded a force of powerful warriors (p. 32).

But her observation seems to have gone unnoticed.

The position of the Ìyálôde (lit., "mother in charge of external affairs") is widely known, but as Bolanle Awe[12] has recently (1974) shown, has been widely misinterpreted. Interest in the economic position of Yoruba women has overshadowed their political importance, so that the Ìyálôde have been regarded as heads of mutual aid associations (Lebeuf 1963:113) or of organizations of market women. In fact, in the pre-colonial era these women held great political power in several Yoruba kingdoms; the Ìyálôde was "in a complementary position" to the Ọba and his male chiefs, and was often referred to as Òtun Ọba, "the King's right hand" (Awe 1974:16). Specific functions of the Ìyálôde differed from one kingdom to another, but Dr. Awe has put together the following general attributes of the office:

> She was, like the male chiefs, also a chief in her own right and had her own special insignia of office . . . her own personal servants and her special drummers and bell ringers to call the women to attention. Her title was an all embracing one which gave her jurisdiction over all women . . . she did not have to belong to a special social class to attain her position. Her most important qualifications were her proven ability as a leader, able to articulate the feelings of the women, her control of vast economic resources to maintain her new status as a chief and her popularity . . . As a spokesman she was given access to all positions of power and authority within the town. She was present at all levels of policy making within the state, exercising with the chiefs in their council legislative, judicial and executive powers . . . To coordinate all women's interests, she had her own Council of subordinate chiefs who exercised similar functions over the women as the main Council of Chiefs (pp. 4-5).

Discussing the military role of the Ìyálôde of the Ẹgba area, Abraham (1958:333) notes, "it was a woman's duty to see that her husband was well provided with food, weapons and ammunition. A rich Ìyálôde used to ensure that all the warriors of her township had the best guns Lagos could produce." Probably the most famous Ìyálôde was Madame Tinubu of Abeokuta, who "supported the whole Abeokuta army." Tinubu's supportive role in the Egba victory over the Dahomean forces in 1851 is discussed by Ajayi and Smith (1964:39). The Ìyálôde system of Oyo was re-established in the several new settlements formed by refugees from that kingdom. Ajayi and Smith (1964:87) mention the role of the Ìyálôde of Ibadan in supplying her troops for the Ijaye wars of 1860. And Awe (1974:9) reports that a candidate for the position of Ìyálôde of Ibadan

> would have to prove her mettle which was often based on her contribution to the military success of the town. The first Iyalode, Iyaola, was said to have made generous contributions to Ibadan war efforts by fielding her own soldiers and giving liberal credit facilities to the war chiefs to enable them to acquire guns and ammunition.

Awe goes on to mention that the Ìyálôde of Ibadan became so important that "she was one of the signatories to the crucial agreement of 1893 which virtually handed over Ibadan administration to the British, and in 1912 an Iyalode acted as regent in Ibadan for a few months after the death of the ruler."

The position of the Ìyálôde was thus quite a flexible one, adaptable to civil administration in times of peace and to military organization and command in times of war. There should now remain no doubt of the potential power and influence of the Ìyálôde, and it would seem quite reasonable to suggest that holders of this office were the models for the armed females of Esie.

An Alternative to Militarism

In the first page of this book, and earlier in this chapter, I indicated that many of the Esie images are "armed, as if for war". A militaristic explanation for the armaments they carry is, indeed, a logical one. However, it is just possible that the representation of arms was intended to signify something quite different. Earlier in this chapter we noted that there is a strong correlation between sex and the type of weapons carried: quivers, bows, and daggers are found only on the male figures; the cutlass is, with only a few exceptions (HT 1, for example) a female accoutrement. Based on this fact, and on reference to

at least one motif found elsewhere in West African artistic traditions, the suggestion has been made that these accoutrements may simply signify male and female economic and cosmological roles.[13]

Hunting is everywhere a men's activity, and the armed Esie males are properly equipped for hunting. But a significant part of farm labor is carried out by women, and the cutlass, a versatile tool, is sometimes used in farming, particularly in the construction of yam mounds, in the harvesting of yams, and in the scraping and cutting of yams after the harvest. The yam is important in both the subsistence and the cosmology of West African forest-dwellers. Moreover, women, fertility, and the earth and its products are universally associated.

These considerations, and the fact that the majority of the armed Esie females hold their cutlasses raised, prompt our reference to representations of Alá, the Earth deity and primordial Mother of the Owerri Ibo. Alá is enshrined in the ornate mbari houses; she is the central purpose in their construction, and mud sculptures of her are central to each shrine (see fig. V. 25). As Herbert Cole (1969a:8) describes her, she is always represented in a regal, authoritative posture, her full breasts prominent, sitting erect with

> her symbolic knife held high in ambivalence, as a warning and a promise to her people. With it she will "peel yams for her children," provide for them.

Photographs of several representations of Alá accompany Cole's three articles on mbari and other symbolic forms of the Owerri Ibo (Cole 1969a, 1969b, 1969c).

But Alá combines other attributes as well, and Cole's further description, quoting some of his Ibo informants, calls to mind attributes of the Yoruba Ìyálôde. Speaking still of her raised cutlass, he says,

> with it she will 'direct her crowds' and 'guide her people'. And with it she 'will kill her offenders, Bwim! and swallow them up'. . . . Her leg bangles, intricate body painting, and especially her elaborate headdress show her a rich titled woman, proud, ostentatious, and grand."

I have been able to discover some further aspects of the position of Alá in Owerri cosmology.[14] She is the principal female deity, and the overseer of all welfare. A common phrase reveals her broad functions: Alá chere anyì, "Alá protects us." Chere, "to protect," derives from nche, "to watch over." The sort of "protection" Alá offers is thus very broad, but it is principally military protection. Her cutlass sym-

V.25. Mud sculpture of Alá and her "children" in an *mbari* house at Ndiama Obube, near Owerri. The significance of her regal posture and raised cutlass have prompted suggestions of a symbolism inherent in the armed female figures at Esie.

bolizes her constant readiness to retaliate, swiftly and decisively, against any who would harm her "children." It has no specific significance in any agricultural symbology.

As the principal female deity, *Alá* is paramount over a number of lesser deities with specialized functions, including *Ahanjóku*, goddess of the farm. A symbol of her position *is* the yam-knife, and a girl who has been pledged to her service after her parents have consulted the diviner is called *mma-ji*, "the yam knife." Wooden figures of *Ahanjóku* are placed before yam-sheds, and in village shrines. These do not hold knives; rather, small, real knives are stuck vertically into the tops of their heads.

Reference to *Alá* is made here for comparison, and because it is a purpose of this book to consider all suggestions that have been offered regarding the origin and purpose of the Esie images. But I think that the suggestion that the armed females of Esie embody a female-earth-agriculture concept is tenuous at best. The armed males could, indeed, be hunters; but I would be happier with the idea that the females are

associated with farming and the earth if some of them were equipped with hoes, the tool most widely used in cultivation. But none of the Esie images carries a hoe.

A Pause for Assessment

So where are we? In the foregoing sections of this chapter we have examined various suggestions of origin and purpose of the Esie stones, drawing from a rather large body of what I have called "soft data:" suggestions made from analyses of various oral traditions; comparisions with motifs found in other West African artistic traditions; certain traits such as facial marks, body adornment, weaponry, stool types, etc., and their parallels as recorded in the ethnographies and histories of contemporary populations; and certain possible symbolic and cosmological interpretations of some of these features as they are found in the Esie collection. The result has been a long and detailed process of elimination. I have offered few positive conclusions; I have, in fact, done little more than to systematically dismiss *all* suggestions and possibilities thus far offered.

But there exist other avenues of potentially fruitful investigation, mainly in the areas of geology and archaeology, which can offer "hard" data, and through which at least part of the mystery of the stone images of Esie can be solved. The remaining sections of this chapter will examine the potential of such lines of research, and will conclude with the prediction that the trail of the mystery will eventually lead to the area of Old Ọyọ.

The Source of the Stone

One particularly challenging aspect of the Esie mystery is the source of the stone itself. It obviously took a great quantity of soapstone, of a consistency suitable for carving, to produce the collection. I was shown some samples from Agbanda, a few kilometres to the south; investigations there revealed only a few small outcrops. Construction of a line of the Nigerian Railways near Offa in the early part of this century allegedly exposed a quantity of talc schist, but I have been unable to obtain confirmation of this report. Indeed, it is puzzling that a quarry of the size necessary to cut blocks from which possibly all of the 1000 images might be carved, has not been discovered. To be sure, no search specifically for such a quarry has been conducted, but by 1964 the Geological Surveys of Nigeria had mapped the known mineral deposits over nearly the whole country. Their efforts were halted by the political troubles of 1965 which led to the outbreak of the War of Biafran Secession in 1967. Fig. V. 26, adapted from the Geological Surveys map,[15] shows the known, and projected, deposits of metamorphic rock of the sort in which talc schists are likely to occur.

In the western part of the country two major belts of such schists extend northward almost from the coast, stopping several kilometres from the river Niger and re-appearing again several kilometres to the north. Such schists appear predictably, having formed in basement rock and often along fault lines, and from the patterns of outcroppings inferences can be drawn regarding their subterranean extensions. It can be said with a fair degree of certainty that these deposits extend probably unbroken to the edge of the Niger Valley, but not through the valley, as the stone there is exclusively sedimentary. Logical areas for our search are therefore delineated.

Talc schist can be important economically, finding use in the manufacture of paint, ceramics, rubber, paper, roofing materials, cosmetics, and in a variety of metallurgical applications. The Geological Surveys thus took care to survey and file reports on the larger outcroppings. Of the several reports filed, those dealing with accessible outcrops in closest relative proximity to Esie can be referred to: the Laojo deposits in the Oluwa Forest Reserve, northwest of Okitipupa (Hubbard 1961); a large deposit near Iregun, a village north of Ilesa (De Swardt 1953); the Isanlu Makutu deposit (MacLeod 1963); and several deposits north of the Niger, in Borgu and in areas north of Minna (Truswell 1963). No evidence of any early quarrying activity was reported at any of these sites.

But vast tracts of land remain unsurveyed, and the several thousands of square kilometres within the map coordinates of 8° — 10° N, and 2° — 6° E, much of this at one time or another under the domination of Old Oyo, comprise one such area. Tantalizingly, the projections of the Geological Surveys indicate that significant quantities of schists are likely to be found in these areas. Following the cessation of hostilities in 1970, the efforts of the Geological Surveys were taken up by departments of geology in the major universities. The University of Ibadan assumed the respon-

sibility of completing the job in the western areas, and by 1974 the geology of the Iseyin area had been described, and, predictably, "vast quantities of soapstone" had been reported.[16] Eventually, it can be hoped, the job will be finished. Against that time, we may be able to suggest a method, and provide some preliminary data, that will help to trace the origin of the Esie soapstone.

Talc is a basic magnesium silicate, $Mg_3Si_4O_{10}(OH)_2$, too soft to exist for long in isolation, but the schists in which it occurs comprise other minerals as well. Although the mineralogical composition of a single outcrop of talc schist can vary from one part to another, if sufficient samples from different sections of the same outcrop can be analyzed, that outcrop can be shown to have a "signature," a unique range of proportions of occurrence of certain minerals which resulted from the specific conditions under which it was formed, and which serve to distinguish it from any other. Thus, if all significant outcrops of talc schist were to be systematically analyzed, so that a complete compositional profile could be drawn for each, then the source of a random piece of soapstone, whose mineralogical composition is known, could theoretically be determined. But analysis of outcrops must be rigorously done, so that complete profiles can be drawn. Some samples from surveyed outcrops in Nigeria, in particular the large and possibly economically significant Isanlu Makutu deposit (MacLeod 1963), were subjected to preliminary analysis, but for comparative purposes the results of such analyses give us minimal information. One entry in the G.S.N. Laboratory Report No. 1272, for a sample from Isanlu Makutu, reads: "Talc 97.5%; sillimanite 2.0%; magnetic fraction (mostly iron oxides) 0.5%." The report describes the visual appearance of the sample:

a pale, grey-green, fine-grained rock on fresh surfaces, weathering to a silvery brown-grey; it has an irregularly developed cleavage . . . Under the microscope the talc fraction was found to consist of grains coated by a thin layer of iron oxide. The specimen analyzed was taken from outcrop, and it is probable that this superficial staining does not persist beneath the zone of oxidation.

From this report we can say that the sample is a sillimanite-bearing talc schist of a high degree of purity, and from this conclusion, as we shall see below, we can surmise that Isanlu Makutu was *not* the source for the Esie stone. But we do not know whether the composition of this sample is representa-

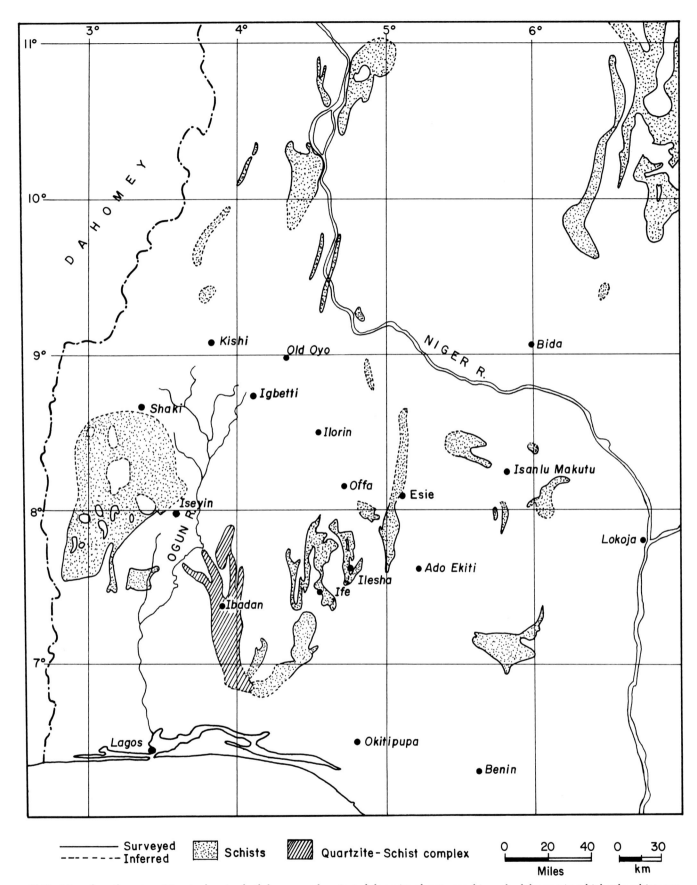

V.26. Map of southwestern Nigeria showing both known and projected deposits of metamorphic rock of the sort in which talc schists are likely to occur. Adapted from a Geological Surveys map of 1964.

tive of the deposit as a whole. Further analysis was recommended by the surveyor, but he indicated that it should not be considered a priority by the Geological Surveys, as the lessee of the land, apparently attracted by the economic potential of the deposit, intended to have it done himself. So far as I know, it was not done.

But if the pieces of the puzzle are to be reassembled, the composition of the Esie stone must be known as well. Analysis would yield results against which future geologists could compare samples of naturally-occurring stone; but an immediate conclusion could be drawn regarding another pressing question: was the Esie stone derived from a common source, or from a number of sources? In the summer of 1974 I collected 15 unidentifiable fragments of stone from Esie, selected visually for varying ranges of colour, texture, and density, and one from Ijara. As there are no fragments at Ofaro, that site could not be represented. These samples were brought to the Department of Geological Sciences at the State University of New York at Buffalo. Operating under a grant from the SUNY Research Foundation, Mr. Stephen A. Hoffman, then an advanced graduate student, selected 10 of these fragments, including the Ijara sample, and subjected them to Heavy Mineral Analysis. Following are portions of his report, submitted in November 1974:

Ten samples of a sillimanite-bearing talc schist from Nigeria were analysed under the following programme to see whether the anthropological history of the statues carved from these rocks could be ascertained.

1. The colour of both fresh and weathered surfaces was determined, using a G.S.A. colour chart.
2. Each sample was crushed fine enough to pass a one phi screen, to attempt to eliminate mineral aggregates.
3. Samples were then placed in a water bath in order to decant off the sizeable clay fraction.
4. Samples were oven dried.
5. Once dry, the samples were sieved for ten minutes to obtain a standard grain size range of between 1 and 2.5 phi.
6. This fraction was then split, using a micro-splitter, to ten grams.
7. Heavy minerals are defined as all minerals having a specific density greater than 2.85. The heavy minerals were separated from the ten gram split using Bromoform (s.d. 2.85).

8. After complete separation, the samples were washed and dried in methanol.
9. The weight of the heavy mineral suite from each sample was determined and recorded.
10. The magnetic population was removed from each heavy mineral suite using a Sepor magnet. The weight of each magnetic population was determined and recorded.
11. The heavy mineral suite, excluding the magnetics, was then split and mounted on a glass slide. Liquid Canada Balsam was used as the mounting medium.
12. 250 grains on each slide were then identified and counted to calculate relative percentages.

These standard sedimentological procedures were employed to determine whether all the samples were derived from the same, or from two or more localities. The anthropologist can then use this information in determining whether the statues were made in one place, or whether they may have been carved in different places and then brought together . . . By studying the heavy mineral suites of the samples, it was thought that this problem could be solved.

Thin-section analysis of the samples was not undertaken due to the small size of the collected fragments and the derivation of more significant data via grain analysis.

A summary of the results is charted in Fig. V. 27. Sample N-10 is from Ijara. Mr. Hoffman's report concludes:

A mineralogical study of the heavy mineral suites of these rocks shows sillimanite to be the major constituent with magnetite and kyanite in varying abundance. Tourmaline, augite, epidote, garnet, and olivine comprise less than 5% of the heavy mineral suite of any particular sample.

Although the heavy mineral suites of all ten samples show little appreciable change, the percent of the heavy mineral population composed of magnetics (magnetite) does show one significant trend. Sample N-10 shows a more weathered surface than all the other samples. Additionally, N-10 has an overwhelming abundance of heavy minerals (greater than 85%) and an equally overwhelming depletion of magnetics (less than .1%) compared to the other samples. This leads one to assume a different source for the rock and consequently, a different area where these statues were made.

However, these rocks are of metamorphic origin which could account for large mineralogical fluctuations over relatively short distances. The evidence for two source areas for the talc schists is but a first approximation, due to the lack of knowledge of the spatial distribution of sillimanite-bearing talc schists in Nigeria.

SAMPLE	FRESH COLOUR	WEATHERED	WT. HEAVY	% HEAVY	WT. MAGN.	% MAGN.	MINERALOGY
N - 1	5Y 8/1 yellowish-grey	10 YR 5/4 mod. yel-brn	.105g	1.05%	.042g	40.0%	60% identifiable 99% sillimanite 1% tourmaline
N - 2	5B 5/1 med. bluish-grey	10 YR 4/2 dk yel-brn	1.632g	16.32%	1.297g	79.47%	61% identifiable 90% sillimanite 9% kyanite 1% augite
N - 3	5G 6/1 greenish-grey	10 YR 4/2 dk yel-brn	.598g	5.98%	.036g	6.02%	42% identifiable 76% sillimanite 24% kyanite
N - 4	5GY 6/1 greenish-grey	10 YR 4/2 dk yel-brn	.231g	2.31%	.156g	67.53%	47% identifiable 75% sillimanite 25% kyanite
N - 5	10 YR 6/2 pale yel-brn	10 YR 5/4 mod. yel-brn	.207g	2.07%	.019g	9.18%	19% identifiable 92% sillimanite 2% kyanite 2% epidote 4% garnet
N - 6	10 YR 6/2 pale yel-brn	10 YR 4/2 dk yel-brn	.332g	3.32%	.112g	33.73%	67% identifiable 87% sillimanite 13% kyanite
N - 7	5Y 8/1 yellowish-grey	10 YR 5/4 mod. yel-brn	.318g	3.18%	.125g	39.31%	35% identifiable 94% sillimanite 55% kyanite 1% garnet
N - 8	10Y 6/2 pale olive	10 YR 5/4 mod. yel-brn	.604g	6.04%	.045g	7.45%	24% identifiable 73% sillimanite 23% kyanite 3% garnet
N - 9	10R 4/6 mod. red-brn	10 YR 5/4 mod. yel-brn	4.954g	49.54%	1.948g	39.32%	35% identifiable 91% sillimanite 7% kyanite 2% garnet
N-10	5Y 7/2 - 5Y 6/4 yel-grey- dusky yellow	10YR 2/2 dusky yel-brown	8.609g	86.09%	.007g	.08%	38% identifiable 95% sillimanite 3% kyanite 1% garnet

V.27. Chart showing results of Heavy Mineral Analysis of nine samples of Esiẹ soapstone (N 1-9) and one from Ijara (N 10). The Ijara sample had a significantly higher percentage of heavy minerals, and lower percentage of magnetics, than any other sample; the proportions of these constituents was so far out of the range of variation of the others to suggest that it derives from a different source.

These results are, to be sure, preliminary. But they are highly promising. Similar methods have been employed successfully in resolving other problems. For example, a Fijian origin of clays used in Tongan pottery has been proven by Light Mineral Analysis. The origin of clays used in the production of pre-Hispanic pottery found in West Mexico is being deduced by the same method.[17] I understand that similar methods have been employed to determine the source of the limestone used in the construction of the Great Pyramid at Gizeh. And, we are gratified to learn, our own underlying hypothesis has been confirmed by at least one successful attempt to trace the origin of *soapstone* artifacts to the quarries which produced the stone. Recognizing that "individual quarries and artifacts from these locations have different concentrations of trace elements because the talcose rocks were formed from a variety of materials under different metamorphic conditions" (Luckenbach, Holland, and Allen 1975:57), two anthropologists and a chemist were able to ascertain precisely the origin of the material used in the production of soapstone pipes and bowls in eastern Virginia during the first two millennia B.C. These researchers recognized the utility of our approach in analyzing a great number of larger fragments, but "mineralogical and major element differences do not permit classification of quarries adequately enough to identify the source of a soapstone artifact such as a pipe or culinary vessel" (p. 57), so they used the more sophisticated technique of determining rare earth element abundances through neutron activation analysis. But their basic hypothesis was the same as ours, and its confirmation shows clearly that such methods have important implications for art history and archaeology. We have indicated that the nine fragments from Esie probably derive from the same source, and that the Ijara stone most likely comes from a different locality. We suggest that by pursuing these methods the source of the stone can be precisely determined.

In the meantime, some tantalizing questions remain. It can be safely assumed that the quarry from which the Esie stone was cut does not lie in the areas to the south of Esie. Otherwise, it would surely have been discovered. Southern Yoruba towns have expanded in geometric progression since the wars of the mid-19th century, and now very few areas that lie between urbanizing centers, and that lie in the paths of the major schist belts, have not been settled, farmed, or tracked. Some towns, such as Ife, Gbongan, and Ibadan have been producers of soapstone images,

but the stone available in these areas is in small quantity.

Quite sparsely settled, however, and only sporadically traversed, is the broad area from the upper Ogun River Valley to the land of Borgu. We have good reason to believe there is soapstone in significant quantity in that area. Somewhere there is a great hole in the ground,[18] and I think it will be found there. Moreover, although we perhaps should not assume that the images were carved on the site where the stone was quarried—as reasonable as this assumption is, there was a production site somewhere. If the carvers regarded the images we know as finished products, given their number and the fragility of the stone there must certainly have been some failures. Some tremendously exciting discoveries are yet to be made.

The Potential of Archaeology

Archaeology, too, has a potentially exciting role to play in solving the mystery. One afternoon during the dry season of 1966 I left my work of repairs to the images and went out of the old House of Images to where some Antiquities Department labourers were digging a ditch for a culvert to run under the road to the parking area. Idly watching the shovel-loads of dirt being tossed out, I suddenly noticed that bits of pottery were being thrown out as well. Work was halted, the ditch was surveyed, and it was found that a clear habitation layer, consisting mainly of pottery fragments, had been exposed at a depth of approximately 46 cm. The layer varied in thickness from 5 to 7 cm. The loose dirt was sifted and as well as a quantity of potsherds, two rounded stones and a broken stone axe (figs. V. 28, 29) were recovered. Examination of the wall of the excavated area behind the new exhibition gallery revealed a similar habitation layer at the same depth (figs. V. 30, 31). Samples of potsherds from all areas where the habitation layer was exposed were deposited with the Department of Archaeology at the University of Ibadan immediately prior to my departure from Nigeria in June 1966.

The land on which the Museum is constructed slopes downward slightly to the north, toward the stream, Osuolo. By the time of my return in July 1974 the site had been graded, and further evidence of former habitation was found at several points, lying now at a depth of only 4 or 5 cm. Potsherds from several of these places were recovered. Near the rain-catch at the north-east corner of the exhibition gallery the upper portion of a large pot was excavated (fig. V. 32), inside of which were found seven oil palm nuts, three shells of a tiny marine snail, and some minute bits of wood and charcoal.

These were exciting discoveries, and they corroborate those portions of the oral traditions which say that the "visitors from the North" settled there for some time. The most popular tradition, as we have discussed on p. 21, states that the visitors sent word to the Elesie that he should stay at home on a particular day to await their visit to the palace to greet him and inform him of their intentions. On that day he went to his okra field instead, and when he returned home the emissaries had already been waiting for some time. The Elesie's story of having been inside the compound preparing refreshment for them was belied by a piece of okra leaf which had stuck to his cheek. The visitors left, enraged, and returned to their encampment, and their petrifaction occurred shortly afterward. But one informant[19] elaborated on this story, to say that the visitors lived at their settlement for some time. "After some years, hunters found the stone images at that place. So the people concluded that the visitors had been turned to stone."

There is no suggestion as to why people left, but it is clear that the site where the images were discovered was inhabited for some time. That the images were associated with the inhabitants of the place is suggested by the fact that *the depth to which many of the images had been covered with earth corresponds precisely to the depth of the artifact layer.*

It would thus be very revealing to determine the dates of occupation of the site. I returned with my samples of organic materials and submitted them to the Nuclear Science and Technology Facility of the State University of New York at Buffalo, for C^{14} dating. The palm nuts seemed the most promising, as

V.28. Two rounded stones and a broken stone axe excavated in 1966 from the culvert under the road to the parking area of the Esie Museum. See also fig. V.29, and refer to fig. I.16 for original locations of these and other artifacts.

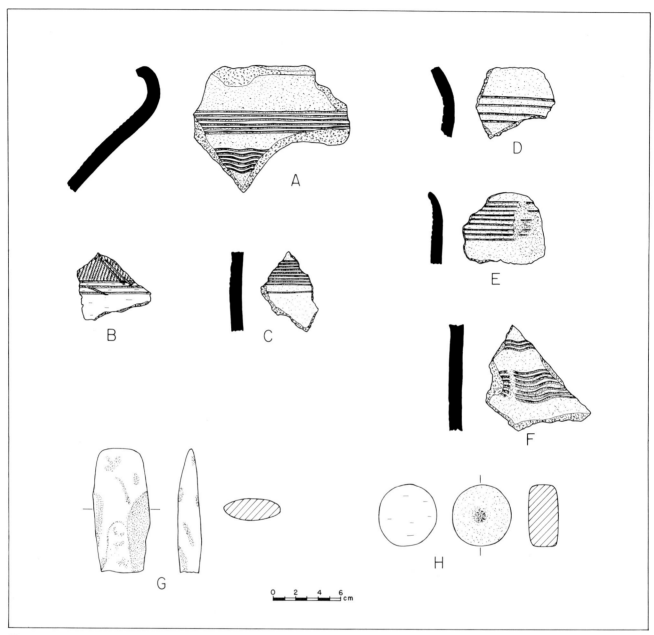

V.29. A-F, potsherds found at a depth of approx. 46 cm. in the sides of the culvert under the access road; G and H, the axe and one of the rounded stones pictured in fig. V.28.

the quantity of charcoal (1.7 grams) and the other materials was too small. Unfortunately, after cleaning, the palm nuts yielded only slightly over 2 grams of datable material, which was insufficient for the Facility's equipment; processing yielded no measurable results.

The Esie site, having been largely cleared and graded, is eminently suitable for thorough archaeological investigation. Analysis of recovered materials will certainly tell us when the site was inhabited, a valuable piece of information from which I think we can logically deduce the time of arrival of the images.

V.30. Potsherds protruding from the earth behind the exhibition gallery, 1974.

V.31. Small pot exposed by erosion of the earth behind the gallery, 1974.

Conclusion: An Ọyọ Connection?

Such investigations may not, however, tell us whence the images came. Throughout this chapter I have been leaning increasingly toward the suggestion of an Old Ọyọ origin of the stones. Some archaeological investigations were conducted at Old Ọyọ by Frank Willett (1959a, 1959b, 1961) during the 1956-57 season, and are currently being continued by Robert Soper of the University of Ibadan. Mr. Soper saw my Esiẹ potsherds and advised me (personal communication, July 1976) that they resembled none of the pottery types either he or Willett had found at Old Ọyọ.

But it seems to me highly plausible that the city of Old Ọyọ itself, or some area under its immediate domination, or one of the neighbouring towns at one time or another occupied by refugees from the city, was the site of origin of the Esiẹ stones. I hope that geology and archaeology will eventually prove me correct; in the meantime we can summarize the bases for this suggestion.

I have shown, through a process of systematic elimination, that it is unlikely that the Esiẹ images came from any of the well-known centres of artistic productivity. Not only is there no conclusive stylistic similarity, but there is the problem of the availability

79

V.32. Rim of large pot, excavated in 1974 at the northeast corner of the exhibition gallery. The scale is approx. 31 cm.

of the requisite quantity of steatite. I have also demonstrated that the numerous "theories" of origin of the images have been based on very weak, if not erroneous, premises. Having thus eliminated all other possibilities, and still faced with the problem, our search is inevitably narrowed to the old Yoruba kingdom of Ọyọ (Ọ́yọ́ Ilé, "Home Ọyọ," called *Katunga* in Hausa). And there are several indicators which suggest this to be a strong possibility.

In the first place, we know that the Ọyọ were prolific sculptors. Captain Hugh Clapperton, on his visit to the city in 1826, reported that

> The people of Katunga are fond of ornamenting their doors, and the posts which support their verandahs, with carvings; and they have also statues or figures of men and women, standing in their court yards. The figures carved on their posts and doors are various, but principally of the boa snake, with a hog or antelope in his mouth; frequently men taking slaves, and sometimes a man on horseback leading slaves (1829:48).

Unfortunately, he gives us no description of the "statues or figures of men and women," nor does he indicate whether any were stone. Later (p. 58) he

observed that "the posts supporting the verandahs and doors of the king's and caboceers' houses are generally carved in bas relief, with figures representing the boa killing an antelope or a hog, or with processions of warriors attended by drummers. The latter are by no means meanly executed . . ." Robert Soper has recovered one large and quite well preserved wooden post carved with figures of people and animals; this is now in the Department of Archaeology at the University of Ibadan. Of course, we cannot know the age of Clapperton's figures, and Soper had not yet been able to date his post, but these constitute evidence of a highly developed artistic tradition which most probably has a long history.

The most persuasive arguments for an Old Ọyọ origin of the Esie stones are to be found in the great variety of elements in the images themselves. As Milburn (in Daniel 1937:49) and Clarke (1938:108) have noted, the images "seem to represent types from a country where various influences meet, and this would seem to indicate a position near the Niger." Indeed so. As we have shown in detail earlier in this chapter, many elements converge in the images. The aberrant head (H 546) suggests a Benin affinity. The figure on the looped stool (T 458) could only have been inspired by Ifẹ. The largest figure (HT 58) bears facial marks that are distinctly Nupe. Some facial marks have been attributed to Borgu. And many northern elements are to be found in headgear, weaponry, and cephalic features.

The best available evidence suggests that Yoruba habitation of Oyọ began sometime in the fourteenth century (Smith 1969:35). According to tradition, another people, ruled by one Egboro, were living there at the time.[20] Òrányàn (also called Òránmíyàn), the youngest son of Odùduwà, journeyed there during the great dispersal of Odùduwà's progeny from Ifẹ. Òrányàn called the place Oyọ", referring to a "slippery place" (from yò, "to slip") where his horse had lost its footing. Òrányàn established his son Àjàká on the throne, then went to live for some years at a place called Oko, and eventually returned to Ifẹ. Àjàká ceded the throne to his more energetic younger brother, Sàngó (later to become the powerful god of thunder and lightning), who was able to wrest total control of the place from Egboro's people.

Although Oyọ was situated near two warlike and threatening peoples, the Borgu and Nupe, its rocky surroundings provided a natural fortress, and it became a commercial centre, receiving influence from all points of the compass. As Smith (1969:34-5) has noted,

> It was strategically placed athwart the tracks which led from the southern forests and across the nearby Niger towards the markets of the West Sudan...traditions indicate that Oyọ maintained close relations—which might frequently become hostile—with its northerly non-Yoruba neighbours, the Hausa, Nupe, and Borgu, the first of whom, at least, were in turn in touch with the distant Arab and Berber across the Sahara. This must have been as much a stimulus as a danger; both trade and warfare would serve to bring the political, military, and technical ideas of the Sudan and even beyond to the Oyọ and through them to the other Yoruba.
>   Thus the state of Oyọ came to be firmly established as a power in northern Yorubaland, at a period which can be provisionally and tentatively assigned to the fourteenth century.

Akinjogbin (1971:311) suggests, however, that the founding of Oyọ could have been as early as the *tenth* century. Regarding the kingdom's favourable position in the trans-Saharan trade, he adds:

> Oyọ appears to have had certain initial advantages, and also to have been exposed early to

certain adversities. Both these conditions eventually aided its growth. First it was situated in the savannah region just south of the River Niger. It therefore seems to have benefited from the trans-Saharan trade, perhaps as early as the fourteenth century...Almost certainly, Oyọ benefited from the trans-Saharan trade during the period of the Songhai ascendency.

After about one hundred years Oyọ was attacked by Nupe and the *Aláfin*, Onigbogi, and many of his people were obliged to flee the city. Onigbogi and his retinue went north to Borgu, but many others, it should be noted, dispersed southward and established or augmented several towns throughout the upper Ogun River valley (cf. Smith 1964)[21] and as far as the forest zone and even into the forests. Thus began approximately 75 years of exile, a period which Smith (1965) has painstakingly reconstructed, during which six *Aláfin* reigned.

The Borgu people were cordial toward Onigbogi, who settled at a place called Gbere (possibly Gberegburu), and died there. He was succeeded by his eldest son Ofinran, during whose reign relations with his hosts deteriorated, so that he decided to return to Yoruba country. Here follows a curious episode, as related to Smith by a chief of Ṣaki:

> By then the hostility of the Borgu had become so great that . . . the move had to be accomplished by a ruse, the Alafin ordering a Nupe man at his court, called Agbomati, to carve models of archers which were placed in position in the bush behind Gbere so as to seem to cover the Oyọ evacuation. The Borgu, discovering that the Oyọ had gone, pursued them on their path, but they were deceived into firing their arrows at the dummy archers, only realizing that they had been tricked when later in the day crows began to alight on their supposed enemy (Smith 1965:63).

I do not mean to suggest that these "dummy archers" were in any way associated with the images at Esiẹ; moreover, Smith was unable to obtain verification of this story elsewhere. But he notes that Agbomati was subsequently appointed by the *Aláfin* as Oloje, "ruler of the Oje people." The present Oloje "lives with his people at Aha, some ten and a half miles south-east of Shaki" (1965:63, n. 18); the *orìkì* (a praise-name describing attributes worthy of emulation by its bearer) of the Oloje refers to his reputation as a wood-carver for the *Aláfin*. The story does, at least, lend further support to our recognition that a highly developed carving tradition existed at the time (does it also suggest that the tradition was introduced by Nupe?).

There is some evidence that Ofinran sojourned at Kisi for a time, moving thence to Kusu, some nineteen kilometres to the north-east of Ṣaki. Ofinran died there, and was succeeded by his son, Egunoju. The Nupe were still a threat, and Egunoju moved westward to Ṣaki, where he remained for several years. Eventually the hospitality the Ọyọ were afforded again wore thin, and Egunoju moved and founded Igboho, apparently sometime toward the end of the sixteenth century (Smith 1969:103). Following Egunoju, three Alâfin ruled successively at Igboho: Orọmpọto (who, some traditions say, was a woman), Ajiboyede, and Abipa. Throughout this time the Nupe and Borgu threat continued (during the reign of Ajiboyede the Nupe had pushed as far as Igboho itself), but by the time of Abipa's rule the threat had subsided so that, early in the seventeenth century (Smith 1969:103) Abipa was able to return to Ọyọ.

The kingdom had consolidated itself during its period of exile, and its army had increased in efficiency, so that, as Akinjogbin (1971:312) notes, "Certainly by 1591, when the Moroccans from across the Sahara conquered Songhai and brought that empire to an end, Ọyọ was in a position strong enough to benefit from the ruins." From this time until early in the 19th century, despite extreme internal political instability (Law 1971), Ọyọ expanded to its greatest power and size, conquering portions of Borgu and Nupe to the north, Dahomey to the south-west, and extending its influence over many southern kingdoms, even to the coast. The kingdom maintained its boundaries up through the peaceful and prosperous reign of Abiọdun (1774-1789). But Abiọdun's reign of peace seems to have weakened his army, and Ọyọ's frontiers became increasingly vulnerable. A devastating defeat by Borgu in 1783, and another by Nupe in 1791 precipitated the inexorable decline in the kingdom's power and influence. The declaration of independence of Afọnja, the Arè-Ọnà-Kakànfò (military commander-in-chief), at Ilọrin in about 1817 gave the Fulani an unshakeable foothold in that town, and the events leading up to the final fall of Ọyọ at the hands of the Fulani in about 1837 are well documented (cf. Smith 1969:133-154).

Against this historical reconstruction, let us return finally to the Esiẹ images. They may or may not represent a king and his court, as some writers have suggested. But whether or not the image revered as the Ọba Èrè was intended to represent a king, courtly elements are evident, most notably in the presence of the Ìlàrí, the royal servants and messengers who were first used in Ọyọ. We have suggested that the armed females most likely represent the Ìyálôde, another Ọyọ institution. Daniel (1937:47) recorded suggestions by the Àwòrò that some of the images are dressed and coiffured like the Mágbà, the priests of Sàngó. Sàngó, as we know, was an early Alâfin of Ọyọ (regardless of whether or not he was a Bariba of Borgu, as some sources state), and his worship began there. The presence of non-Ọyọ elements can easily be explained by the fact of Ọyọ's long existence as an important commercial centre. As well as receiving continual influence from the north, the kingdom maintained connections with Benin, and with its parent Ife, as we know from the journals of Clapperton (1829) and the Landers. Richard and John Lander, in fact, purchased a fragment of an Ife glass-bead crucible in the market at Ọyọ (Hallett 1965:89, citing information provided by Frank Willett). Ọyọ, indeed, was quite a cosmopolitan city, which flourished due to its favourable position in the North-South trade.

The most plausible conclusion to be drawn from the various Esiẹ traditions is that the images were there before the Igbomina settlers, under Baragbon, migrated into the area in the late 18th century. Let us review the following facts, and consider some interpretations of these facts. There is evidence of habitation of some duration on the site. Many of the images were covered by earth to the same depth as the habitation layer. The images had been subjected to considerable willful destruction—again, apparently, before the arrival of the inhabitants of Esiẹ. The Esiẹ people did not inflict such extensive damage upon the images. Neither could it have occurred as a result of the Ijaye wars of the mid-nineteenth century, during which the Esiẹ people fought against the Ibadan.[22] Although the Ibadan pushed north as far as Offa (Ajayi and Smith 1964:69), no battles were fought in the near vicinity of Esiẹ. But our recovery of innumerable soapstone fragments from the site, all of which were found just where the images had stood, and most of which were recovered from beneath the surface, demonstrates conclusively that the damage was inflicted there.

The precise age of the images may never be known. Tangential evidence, however, suggests that they are quite old. Several terra-cotta figures, discussed and illustrated in Chapter IV, were found with them. Two fragments of these were subjected to thermoluminescent dating at Oxford in 1974. One fragment was a small smoothly-curved piece which very likely came from a hollow human or animal figure; it resembled some of those in fig. IV. 5, and was assigned the reference number TC 39. The other showed no diagnostic features, and was referred to simply as "orange clay nodule." In a letter dated 20 January 1975 Professor Thurstan Shaw sent me the following results and offered his speculation as to their significance:

Ref. TC 39   890 ± 75 years (± 10 error)
Ref. 'orange clay
    nodule'   770 ± 70 years (± 10 error)

Dr. S. J. Fleming comments: 'In light of the errors there is no reason to suggest these are not contemporary'.

I find these results interesting as, although I feel that thermoluminescent dating needs a lot more validation before one can place as much reliance on it as one now can on radiocarbon, a date of around A.D. 1100 for the Esie terracottas would fit in with the current dating picture for Ife.

To be sure, we cannot be certain that the terra-cottas were produced within the same time period as the stone images, nor that they derive from the same cultural tradition, nor even that they were brought to their present site together with the images. But there is no evidence to suggest an alternative to any of the above. Indeed, as we have indicated in Chapter IV, two of the terra-cotta heads show striking resemblances to four of the stone heads, and it is interesting that these four are among the six which were indisputably complete as heads. Moreover, as Willett (1959b) has shown, there apparently was a tradition of terra-cotta sculpture at Old Oyo.

But there are other suggestions for the antiquity of the stone images. For example, we know that the expansion of Oyo in the eighteenth century was due largely to its efficient cavalry. Why is no horse represented in the Esie collection? Other animals are represented. If the images are faithful representations of various cultural elements of their period, as it seems they are, then we can only conclude that they were produced *before* the adoption of the horse and the use of cavalry by the Oyo, which most probably occurred in the sixteenth century (Law 1975). Further, throughout the eighteenth century gunpowder and muskets were increasingly used by the Oyo, but none of the images carries a firearm.

So, on the basis of all the foregoing, I will take the liberty of offering the following reconstruction of the history of the Esie stone images:

Oyo, at least by the fourteenth century, was a flourishing commercial centre, receiving steady influence from both north and south. Soapstone images were carved to represent both Oyo elements and those from areas of commercial contact; they represented a microcosm of the internal and external world of the Oyo. In the fifteenth century the Nupe attacked and conquered the city. The Alâfin and his court fled north to Borgu, beginning the long period of exile reconstructed by Smith (1965). But others dispersed southwards, establishing new settlements even as far as the forests in the southern parts of Yorubaland (Smith 1965:63). One such migration was effected by the group into whose care the images had been entrusted.

By this time the images had come to be regarded as symbolic of the values and fortunes of the Oyo kingdom; indeed, they represented Oyo itself. They had to be preserved. The great majority were easily portable, but some weighed over 50 kg., and the largest (HT 58) weighed considerably more than its present 104 kg. But, probably with the help of litters, they managed to convey the images about 185 kilometres to the south-east, eventually settling at the wooded site near the present village of Esie. This was a suitable place for a temporary settlement. Although it offered no natural defenses, it was near a constant source of water, and the surrounding savannah was fertile. And there they lived for some years, protecting their images, seeking, in fact, to maintain the glory that was and possibly could be again.

But the Nupe relentlessly continued to expand. We do not know the limits of this expansion, but Eyo (1974) has suggested that it reached as far as Ife and Owo.[23] Our small settlement of Oyo refugees, its inhabitants having insufficient advance warning, was easily overrun. Two images were saved, their bearers reaching the area of Ofaro where they deposited them under the protective rock overhang.[24] But the people had no choice but to abandon the others, which were brutally assaulted by the invading Nupe. Many were beheaded, many inflicted with deep cuts, many were gouged about the eyes and mouth, suggesting that the vandals saw in them a significance greater than that presented by mere carved stone. Some of those who fled this onslaught settled somewhere in the area of Ijara, where they carved crude facsimiles of their former charges. The others either were killed or enslaved by the Nupe, or were too widely dispersed ever to re-group. And so the images remained until they were discovered by the later Igbomina migrants. (It is interesting to speculate that, if Esie tradition, as recorded in the *Itan Esie*, is reasonably accurate, the ancestors of these migrants also left Oyo as a result of that city's sack by the Nupe in the mid-sixteenth century.)

An alternative version to this might state that the images were produced during the "Igboho Period" of Ọyọ history, when the exiled Alâfin sojourned at Kiṣi, Kusu, Ṣaki, and Igboho. We know (Smith 1965) that the successive kings who ruled during this period were often threatened by Nupe, who at one point penetrated as far as Igboho itself, and that there were several migrations away from the parent group. One such migrating group could have borne the images to their present site. We know, too, that there is abundant talc schist in this area. But such an alternative possibility would not alter the events which were to occur over the next several decades: that the images were conveyed to their present site by Ọyọ emigrants sometime during the fifteenth or early sixteenth century, and that those people were attacked and driven away from their settlement, and their images vandalized, by the expanding Nupe.

Great strides have been made over the past decade in the reconstruction of the early history of the states of West Africa, especially of the history of Ọyọ. Most of such historical reconstructions have been based on oral traditions, and this method still has its critics. But (cf. Vansina 1965 and Stevens 1978) when several traditions of the same happenings are collected from disparate sources, with the researcher being reasona-bly sensitive to the nuances of the language of trans-mission, when account is taken of the mode and motive of transmission and of the possibility of politi-cal and chronological distortion, and when each is then compared in detail with the others, elements of oral tradition can often be seen to offer the promise of veracity to even the most conservative historian. Most of those several historians cited in this chapter have carefully weighed and compared their data before setting them down in print. And when these sources are subjected to careful perusal, equally careful atten-tion being paid to interpretations drawn by eth-nologists and art historians, as I have tried to do in this book, the account of the possible history of the Esiẹ stone images which I have reconstructed above emerges as more than conjecture.

The reader need not accept the suggestions offered here. He may—indeed, he should—await the results of further geological and archaeological investiga-tions. I await them too. I am confident that such further investigations will prove me at least roughly correct; but I am prepared to be proven dead wrong. In the meantime, this book is offered as what I hope will be a vital research tool for those who might wish to pursue further the mystery of the Stone Images of Esiẹ.

Notes, Chapter V

[1] Ethnological investigations were conducted in parts of Adamawa and southern Sardauna Provinces of the upper Benue River valley, from September 1969 through March 1971.

[2] Ṣàngó worship originated in Ọyọ, whence it was brought southward by successive waves of emigration from that city. It did not take hold in Ifẹ, whose inhabitants revere a vengeful god associated with thunder and lightning, called Òrámfè. But Òrámfè's attributes are similar to Ṣàngó's, both are also called Jàkúta ("The Stone-Thrower"), and both may be projections of a common notion.

[3] Based on an interview she conducted in 1946 with the Asebuhene (King of the Asebu), Nana Amanfi III, and some of his elders.

[4] In a letter to me, dated 1 December 1974, Mrs. Meyerowitz wrote, "I wish that when you have finished with the Esie stone figures, you would do some research on the 'stone' figures in Ghana which so far are only a legend. There are said to be many more than the ones I mentioned in the 'Silent Grove'. For instance, on an island near the mouth of the Tano river; I had permission from the chief to see these figures but the priestess in charge would not hear of it." On pp. 66-7 of her *Akan Traditions of Origin* (1952) she records reports of stone figures in other areas. There might be something here for future researchers.

[5] W. Fagg (1959) suggests that this head (H 546) might have come from an unusually large figure. In fact, this is one of six heads which were carved complete *as* heads; the others are H 128, 244, 245, 370, and 545.

[6] It may be only coincidence, but in areas of Ifẹ influence Èṣù seems frequently associated with sacred stone carvings. He himself is often represented in stone. A squat granitic figure of Èṣù sits near the entrance to the shrine of Oluorogbo in Ifẹ, and Allison (1964) recorded a fine example in Igbajo.

[7] But Abraham (1958:680) gives a tradition that she is the wife of Òrànyàn and the mother of Ṣàngó, and of Sòpònó, the dread god of smallpox. Other traditions list her as the daughter of Odùduwà given in marriage to Obàtálá, or as the daughter of Obàtálá (cf. Dennett 1910:97ff.). In any case, she is the water spirit worshipped elsewhere in Yorubaland as Yemoja; and the sea goddess revered as Yemanja in Brazil and elsewhere in the New World. Compare the image of Yemoo with the carved wooden image of Yemanja in Bahia, as published by Verger (1954:pl.118).

[8] This is one of the famous "Tsoede Bronzes" of Tada, allegedly left there by the Nupe culture hero Tsoede (see Nadel 1942:72-6; Willett 1967:168-173; see also Smith 1965:61 for the possibility of Tsoede's participation in the sixteenth-century Nupe sack of Ọyọ). I took this photograph in Tada in 1965. Recently this figure, and its six companions—three human figures, two ostriches, and one elephant—have been removed to the National Museum, Lagos.

[9] This is a large equestrian statue allegedly representing "Elempe, King of the Nupe," (the maternal grandfather of Ṣàngó, according to some traditions). Since Independence it has stood in the National Museum; the one now in the palace of the Òràngún is a copy.

[10] See n. 6.

[11] In any case, Akinjogbin (1971:337), in discussing the subsequent demise of Dahomey, notes that "the Dahomeyan army had been weakened by a long period of peace and consequent lack of practice."

[12] I am grateful to Dr. Awe for her kind permission to cite and to quote from her 1974 paper.

[13] Professor Leon Siroto made this suggestion after I had summarized some of my findings in a lecture to the University Seminar on Primitive and Pre-Columbian Art, Columbia University, January 16, 1976. The invitation to lecture before this group was extended by Professor Douglas Fraser.

[14] My thanks go to Mr. Linus Okere, of Nnorie, Ngor-Okpala, Owerri Division, for this information. Mr. Okere is a graduate student in anthropology at the State University of New York at Buffalo, and is personally familiar with the *mbari* houses, and their cosmology, in his home area.

[15] This map is adapted by permission of the Federal Ministry of Lands and Surveys, Geological Surveys Division.

[16] As reported to me in July 1974 by Dr. M. O. Ọyawoye, Chairman of the Department of Geology, University of Ibadan, one of whose students had completed a thesis on the geology of the Iseyin area.

[17] I was informed of the Polynesian research by Dr. Charles Cazeau, who was unable to locate the precise reference, published in *Science*. The West Mexican research is being conducted by Dr. Cazeau, and by Dr. Stuart Scott, at the State University of New York at Buffalo.

[18] But Philip Allison, in his review of the final draft of the manuscript for this book (December 1976), reminded me of another possibility:

It may be relevant that T. A. Joyce ("Steatite Figures from Sierra Leone in the British Museum," *Man*, 1909) records that he was told by Major Anderson, a District Commissioner, that he had visited a steatite working consisting of a fifteen foot long tunnel, driven into the side of a hill, in which fragments of Nomoli carvings were found. One figure which had been carved *in situ* was still attached to the rock. Gallery working of this sort may well be more difficult to locate than an open quarry.

[19] Enoch Afolayan, Chief Petu of Esiẹ, in an interview conducted August 6, 1974.

[20] The date of habitation by ancestors of the Yoruba may well have been earlier than Smith's date; in any case, Willett's (1959a) excavations at Ọyọ have shown that there was an earlier habitation of the site, possibly by Neolithic hunters who periodically took shelter in a large cave there.

[21] Earlier thought had been that such towns, most of them hill communities, were established following the final collapse of Ọyọ in about 1837 (cf. Gleave 1963). But Smith points to evidence which indicates considerably earlier habitation of these sites. His later (1965) researches in the area suggest that many such towns were established following the sixteenth-century flight from Ọyọ before the great Nupe expansion.

[22] As I was informed by the Elesiẹ and a gathering of elders at his palace in July, 1964.

[23] Eva Meyerowitz had earlier (1943:35) suggested that the southernmost expansions of the Nupe Kingdom extended to Ifẹ "and parts of Benin."

[24] This, of course, disregards the Ofaro account. But see Chapter III, n. 1.

Bibliography of References Cited

Abraham, R. C.
1958 *Dictionary of Modern Yoruba.* London: University of London Press.

Ajayi, J. F. Ade, and Robert Smith
1964 *Yoruba Warfare in the 19th Century.* Cambridge: Cambridge University Press in Association with the Institute of African Studies, University of Ibadan.

Akinjogbin, I. A.
1967 *Dahomey and its Neighbours, 1708-1818.* Cambridge: at the University Press.
1971 "The Expansion of Oyo and the Rise of Dahomey, 1600-1800." *History of West Africa.* J. F. Ade Ajayi and Michael Crowder, eds. Vol. I. London: Longman Group (New York: Columbia University Press, 1972).

Allison, Philip A.
1963 "Newly Discovered Stone Figures from the Yoruba Village of Ijara, Northern Nigeria." *Man* LXIII, 115.
1964 "A Carved Stone Figure of Eshu from Igbajo, Western Nigeria." *Man,* July-August, 131, 104-5.
1968 *African Stone Sculpture.* London: Lund Humphries.

Awe, Bolanle
1974 "The Institution of the Iyalode within the Traditional Yoruba Political System." Paper presented at the Seventeenth Annual Meetings of the African Studies Association, Chicago, October 30—November 2.

Bertho, J., and R. Mauny
1952 "Archeologie du pays Yoruba et du Bas-Niger." *Notes Africaines* 56, 97-114.

Bivar, A. D. H.
1964 *Nigerian Panoply: Arms and Armour of the Northern Region.* Department of Antiquities, Nigeria.

Bowen, T. J.
1857 *Adventures and Missionary Labours in Several Countries in the Interior of Africa from 1849 to 1856.* Charleston, N. C.: Southern Baptist Conference.

Burton, Sir Richard F.
1864 *A Mission to Gelele, King of Dahome.* 2 vols. London (edition used: C. W. Newbury, ed.; New York: Praeger, 1966).

Clapperton, Hugh
1829 *Journal of a Second Expedition into the Interior of Africa from the Bight of Benin to Soccattoo.* London: John Murray.

Clarke, J. D.
1938 "The Stone Figures of Esie." *Nigeria Magazine* 14, 106-8.

Cole, Herbert M.
1969a "Mbari is Life." *African Arts/Arts d'Afrique* II, 3, Spring.
1969b "Mbari is a Dance." *African Arts/Arts d'Afrique* II, 4, Summer.
1969c "Art as a Verb in Iboland." *African Arts/Arts d'Afrique* III, 1, Autumn.

Courlander, Harold
1973 "The Stone People of Esie." Chapter 26 of *Tales of Yoruba Gods and Heroes.* New York: Crown Publishers.

Dalzel, Archibald
1793 *The History of Dahomy, an Inland Kingdom of Africa Compiled from Authentic Memoirs.* London: Author.

Daniel, F. de F.
1937 "The Stone Figures of Esie, Ilorin Province, Nigeria." *Journal of the Royal Anthropological Institute* 67, 43-49.
1939 "Stone Sculpture in Nigeria. I. Stone Figures at Ofaro." *Nigeria Magazine* 28, 107-8.

Dennett, R. F.
1910 Nigerian Studies: The Religious and Political System of the Yoruba. London: Macmillan.

De Swardt, A. M. J.
1953 "The Geology of the Country around Ilesha." *Geological Survey of Nigeria, Bulletin No. 23.* Geological Surveys Office, Ibadan.

Elphinstone, K. V., comp.
1921 *Gazetteer of Ilorin Province.* London: Waterlow & Sons (edition used: London: Frank Cass, 1972).

Eyo, Ekpo O.
1974 *Recent Excavations at Ife and Owo and their Implications for Ife, Owo and Benin Studies.* Ph.D. Dissertation, Department of Archaeology, University of Ibadan.

Fagg, Bernard
1956 "A Life-size Terracotta Head from Nok." *Man* LVI, 95.
1959 "The Nok Culture in Prehistory." *Journal of the Historical Society of Nigeria* I, 288-93.

Fagg, Bernard, and William Fagg
1960 "The Ritual Stools of Ancient Ife." *Man* LX, 155.

Fagg, William
1949 "On a Stone Head of Variant Style at Esie, Nigeria." *Man* LIX, 60.

Fagg, William, and Margaret Plass
1964 *African Sculpture.* London: Studio Vista; New York: E. P. Dutton.

Forbes, F. E.
1851 *Dahomey and the Dahomans: Being the Journals of Two Missions to the King of Dahomey, and Residence at his Capital in the Years 1849 and 1850.* London: Longmans, Brown, Green and Longmans.

Forde, Daryll
1955 "The Nupe." *Peoples of the Niger-Benue Confluence.* Ethnographic Survey of Africa, Western Africa, Pt. X. London: International African Institute.

Friend, Donald
1939 "Stone Sculpture in Nigeria. II. Carved Stones at Effon." *Nigeria Magazine* 28, 108-9.

Frobenius, Leo
1913 *The Voice of Africa.* 2 vols. Rudolf Blind, trans. London (edition used; New York: Benjamin Blom, 1968).

Gleave, Michael B.
1963 "Hill Settlements and their Abandonment in Western Yorubaland." *Africa,* XXXIII, October.

Hallett, Robin, ed.
1965 *The Niger Journal of Richard and John Lander.* London: Routledge and Kegan Paul.

Herskovits, Melville J.
1938 *Dahomey: An Ancient West African Kingdom.* 2 vols. New York: J. J. Augustin.

Hubbard, M.
1961 "Laojo Clay and Talc Deposits, Ondo Province." Geological Survey of Nigeria Report. Ms. in Geological Surveys Office, Ibadan.

Idowu, E. B.
1962 *Olódùmàrè: God in Yoruba Belief.* London.

Johnson, Samuel
1921 *The History of the Yorubas from the Earliest Times to the Beginning of the British Protectorate.* London: G. Routledge & Sons.

Jones, Bovell
1936 "The Ikole in the Ekiti Division of the Ondo Province." Government Report, Lagos.

Jones, G. I.
1974 "Social Anthropology in Nigeria during the Colonial Period." *Africa* XLIV, 3, 280-89.

Law, R. C. C.
1971 "The Constitutional Troubles of Ọyọ in the Eighteenth Century." *Journal of African History* XII, 1, 25-44.
1973 "The Heritage of Oduduwa: Traditional History and Political Propaganda among the Yoruba." *Journal of African History* XIV, 2, 207-222.
1975 "A West African Cavalry State: The Kingdom of Ọyọ." *Journal of African History* XVI, 1, 1-15.

Lebeuf, Annie M.D.
1963 "The Role of Women in the Political Organization of African Societies." *Women of Tropical Africa.* Denise Paulme, ed. London: Routledge and Kegan Paul (edition used: Berkeley and Los Angeles: University of California Press, 1971).

Leggatt, Jack
1962 "Report to the Antiquities Department: Stone Sculptured Figures at Ijara." Ms. in the Library of the National Museum, Lagos.

Luckenbach, Alvin H., C. G. Holland, and Ralph O. Allen
1975 "Soapstone Artifacts: Tracing Prehistoric Trade Patterns in Virginia." *Science* 187, 4171, 57-58.

MacLeod, W.
1963 "Memorandum on the Isanlu Makutu Talc Deposit." Geological Survey of Nigeria Report No. 1198. Ms. in Geological Surveys Office, Kaduna.

Meyerowitz, Eva L. R.
1943 "The Stone Figures of Esie in Nigeria." *The Burlington Magazine* LXXXII, 31-36.
1952 *Akan Traditions of Origin.* London: Faber.
1975 *The Early History of the Akan States of Ghana.* London: The Red Candle Press.

Milburn, S.
1936 "Stone Sculptures at Esie (Ilorin Province)." *The Nigerian Teacher* VIII, 2-7.

Murray, K. C.
1951 "The Stone Images of Esie and their Yearly Festival." *Nigeria Magazine* 37, 45-64.

Murray, K. C., and Frank Willett
1958 "The Ore Grove at Ife, Western Nigeria," *Man* LVIII, 87.

Nadel, S. F.
1942 *A Black Byzantium.* London: Oxford University Press for the International African Institute.

Norris, Robert
1789 *Memoirs of the reign of Bossa Ahadee, King of Dahomy, an Inland Country of Guiney. To Which are added, The Author's Journey to Abomey the Capital; and A short Account Of the African Slave Trade.* London.

Oyinloye, Olatunji
1953 "Esie Stone Images." Ms. in the Library of the National Museum, Lagos.

Shaw, Thurstan
1970 *Igbo-Ukwu: An Account of Archaeological Discoveries in Eastern Nigeria.* 2 vols. Evanston, Ill.: Northwestern University Press.

Skertchly, J. A.

1874 *Dahomey As It Is: Being a Narrative of Eight Months' Residence in that Country.* London: Chapman and Hall.

Slye, J.

1962 "The Strange Stone Figures of Ijara, A Puzzling Find in Northern Nigeria." *Illustrated London News* 241, 251-3.

Smith, R. S.

1964 "Erin and Iwawún: Forgotton Towns of the Òkè Ògùn." *Odu*, n.s., 1, 1, July, 17-32.

1965 "The Alafin in Exile: A Study of the Igboho Period in Oyo History." *Journal of African History* VI, I, 57-77.

1967 "Yoruba Armament." *Journal of African History* VIII, 87-106.

1969 *Kingdoms of the Yoruba.* London: Methuen.

Snelgrave, William

1734 *A New Account of Some Parts of Guinea, and the Slave-Trade.* London.

Stevens, Phillips, Jr.

1965 "The Festival of the Images at Esie." *Nigeria Magazine* 87, 1-7.

1966 "Orisha-Nla Festival." *Nigeria Magazine* 90, 183-198.

1975 "The Kisra Legend and the Distortion of Historical Tradition." *Journal of African History* XVI, 2, 185-200.

1978 "The Uses of Oral Traditions in the Writing of African History." *Tarikh*, 6, 1, April. Special Issue on Historical Method. R. S. Smith, ed.

Temple, O., comp. and C. L. Temple, ed.

1919 *Notes on the Tribes, Provinces, Emirates and States of the Northern Provinces of Nigeria.* Cape Town: Argus.

Thompson, Robert Farris

1974 *African Art in Motion: Icon and Act in the Collection of Katherine Coryton White.* Berkeley: University of California Press.

Truswell, J. F.

1963 "The Geology of Parts of Niger and Zaria Provinces, Northern Nigeria." *Geological Survey of Nigeria, Bulletin No. 29.* Geological Surveys Office, Kaduna.

Vansina, Jan

1965 *Oral Tradition: A Study in Historical Methodology.* H. M. Wright, trans. Chicago: Aldine.

Verger, Pierre

1954 *Dieux d'Afrique: Culte des Orishas et Vodouns à l'ancienne Côte des Esclaves en Afrique et à Bahia la Baie de tous les Saints au Brésil.* Paris: Paul Harmann.

Willett, Frank

1959a "Recent Excavations at Old Oyo and Ife, Nigeria." *Man*, June, 135, 99-100.

1959b "A Terra-Cotta Head from Old Oyo, Western Nigeria." *Man* LIX, 286, 180-181.

1961 "Investigations at Old Oyo, 1956-57, An Interim Report." *Journal of the Historical Society of Nigeria* II, 59-77.

1967 *Ife in the History of West African Sculpture.* London: Thames and Hudson; New York: McGraw-Hill.

Index

For the sake of simplicity and uniformity, tonal marks are not indicated. Items mentioned in captions to Text Figures are included without special designation. Certain commonly-mentioned names and terms, e.g., "Esie," "Yoruba," "soapstone," etc., are not indexed.

Okodo, settlement site, 19, 30 (n.4,6)
Olodumare, supreme Yoruba deity, 55
Olofin, son of Odududuwa, 30 (n.3),
    52, 55
Oloje, ruler of Oje people, 81
Olomu, ruler of Omu-Aran town, 19
Olowu, legendary Esie culture hero,
    35, 37
Olu, ruler of Ofaro, 32-34, 40 (n.1)
Olurogbo, Ife deity, 85 (n.6)
Oluwa Forest Reserve, 72
Onigbogi, Alafin, 81
Ora, settlement, 37, 40 (n.3)
Oramfe, Ife deity, 85 (n.2)
Ore Grove, Ife, 53
oriki, Yoruba praise-name, 37, 81
orisa, generic term for Yoruba deities, 22
Orisa Nla, see "Obatala"
Orisa-Oko, Yoruba agriculture deity, 22
Oro, town, x, 2, 22
Orogbesasa, Elesie of Esie, 19
Oruku, settlement site, 37
Osifoluke, S., Antiquities Department
    photographer, xi, 32
Osula, Antiquities Officer, 10
Osuolo, stream, 21, 76
Owerri, Ibo area, 70, 71, 85 (n.14)
Oyedokun, Elesie of Esie, 20, 37
Oyeoka, C., Antiquities Department
    ethnographer, 32, 33
Oyeyipo, J., Elesie of Esie, x, 20, 22, 34
Oyinloye, O., 1, 3, 19. 30 (n.3), 52, 62, 65,
    bibl.

Oba Ere, see "King of the Images"
Oba Keke, Elesie of Esie, 20
Obalale, title of chief priest of Obatala in
    Ife, 57
Obatala, Yoruba creator deity, 22, 57, 60,
    85 (n.7)
Odeyimi, Baale of Esie, 37
Offa, town, 2, 82
Olarinde, Elesie of Esie, 20
Olasupo, Elesie of Esie, 20
Olayinka, Elesie of Esie. 20, 22
Olorun, Yoruba High God, 21
Oni, title of kings of Ife, 52, 59
Orangun, ruler of Ila-Orangun, 55, 60,
    85 (n.9)
Oranmiyan, see "Oranyan"

Oranyan, son of Oduduwa and founder of
    Oyo, 81, 85 (n.7)
Orompoto, Alafin, 82
Osanyin, Yoruba medicine deity, 22
Osin, stream, 19
Owo, town, 10, 83
Oyawoye, M.O., 85 (n.16)
Oyo, old Yoruba kingdom, 19, 20,
    30 (n.3), 41, 51, 55, 59, 63, 67, 68,
    70-72, 79, 80-84, 86 (n.20,21)

Peace Corps, vii, ix
peregun, Yoruba name for a species of
    Dracaena, 3, 17
Parviz, king of Persia, 52
Petu, Esie chieftaincy title, 30 (n.6), 35,
    37, 86 (n.19)
Plass, M., 53, 59, bibl. (see Fagg, W.)
pomtan, Kissi stone carvings, 59, 61
Popo, town, 68

Ramshaw, H.G., 2
Rashid, H.K., Antiquities Officer, 10
Rubenstein, H., collection of African art, 1

sacrifice, 24-27, 32, 33
Sahara, 52, 81
Salami, Aworo of Esie, 22
Sapetu, chief in Ikerre, 54
Sardauna Province, 63
Scott, S., 85 (n.17)
Senufo, people, 63
Shaw, T., x, 60, 83, bibl.
Sherbro, people, 59, 61
Sherbro-Portuguese ivories, vii
Sierra Leone, vii, 59, 61
Simon, A., S.M.A. missionary, 2
Siroto, L., 85 (n.13)
Skertchly, J.A., 67, bibl.
Slye, J., 34, bibl.
S.M.A., Society of Missions to Africa, x, 2
Smith, R.S., 20, 55, 65, 67, 70, 81-84,
    85 (n.8), 86 (n.20,21), bibl.
smithing, 30, 34, 35
Snelgrave, W., 67-69, bibl.
Sobo, area, 52
Songhai, ancient state, 81, 82
Soper, R., x, 79, 80
standing figures, 56, 65

State University of New York, Buffalo, 74,
    77, 85 (n.14)
stools, 1, 33, 34, 56, 59, 65, 66
Sudan, 50, 51, 81
Sunmonu Abikoye Fadolapo II, Elesie of
    Esie, 20
Swahili, 51

Saki, town, 81, 82, 84
Sango, Yoruba deity, 21, 22, 51, 85 (n.2,7)
Sopono, Yoruba deity, 85 (n.7)

Tada, town, 57, 85 (n.8)
talc schist, 71, 72-75, 84
Tano River, 85 (n.4)
Tapa, Yoruba word for Nupe, 62
Tegbesu, king of Dahomey, 68, 69
Temple, O., and C.L., 63, bibl.
Tera, people, 61, 63
terra-cotta, vii, x, 3, 41-48, 53, 60, 82
thermoluminescence, dating technique,
    41, 82, 83
Thompson, R.F., 30 (n.8), bibl.
Tinubu, Iyalode of Abeokuta, 70
Truswell, J.F., 72, bibl.
Tsoede bronzes, 57, 85 (n.8)
tuyères, 30 (n.4), 34, 36

Vansina, J., 84, bibl.
Verger, P., 57, 85 (n.7), bibl.
Virginia, 76
Volavka, Z., vii

war, warfare, 1, 70, 81, 82
weaponry, various types, 1, 49, 65,
    67-71, 83
Whydah, town, 67-69
Willett, F., vii, x, xi, 41, 43, 53, 55-57, 59,
    60, 63, 79, 82, 83, 85 (n.8), 86 (n.20),
    bibl. (see also Murray, K.C., bibl.)
wood carving, vii, 50, 53, 56, 60

Yagba, Yoruba sub-group, 62, 63
Yawa, name for various peoples, 21, 51
Yemanja, var. of Yemoja in Brazil, 85 (n.7)
Yemoja, Yoruba deity of watery places,
    85 (n.7)
Yemoo (see Yemoja), wife of Obatala, 57

Zam, Nupe sub-group, 62

The Plates

Contents

Introduction

The following discussion briefly describes the process of cataloguing, photography, and repairs to the images effected in 1965-66 and 1974.

Cataloguing and Photography

Cataloguing began in February 1965 with the loose heads. These were arbitrarily classified according to hairstyle and headgear, and these features proved quite effective as classificatory devices; many physiognomic features were found to correlate quite closely with them, as will be seen in the Plates. The complete figures were classified similarly, and "style-groups" emerged which perhaps represent different individual carvers or "schools" of carvers. All features of each head and complete figure were described and measured and recorded in four large notebooks. This resulted in a mass of data which proved far too unwieldy for inclusion in this book. The broad categories used in classifying the heads and complete figures are listed in the Introduction to the Heads section.

As many of the images still bore the dried remains of lichens, roots, or earth, all objects — with the exception of the terra-cottas and the King — were carefully washed with plain water and a soft brush. Every item showing any diagnostic feature at all received a catalogue number. This was written in India ink on a small swatch of white enamel paint which was applied to an out-of-the-way area of the object. The number was then covered with a layer of clear varnish. In the case of the terra-cottas, described and illustrated on pp. 41-48, numbers were written directly on the objects.

With the exception of limb fragments, every numbered object was then photographed. Photography was conducted in the open courtyard of the old House of Images, and was dependent upon sunlight. A woven mat was hung from ropes as a backdrop for the larger objects; the heads and smaller fragments were photographed against a small woven mat draped over a chair. This method produced results which were satisfactory for the compilation of a catalogue, which was the original intention; but both the images and the mats were of a similar beige colour, and both were heavily textured, and unless the sunlight was direct and intense the results often showed resolution insufficient for publication. This was the primary reason for my return in 1974. The Department of Antiquities provided a wooden backdrop which we painted with flat blackboard paint. All of the complete figures and many of the torsos were re-photographed against this background. Several of the heads and smaller objects, including the terra-cottas, were re-photographed against a black cloth.

Repairs

We had been able to replace several heads on torsos before numbering, but because the production of a photographic record was the first priority, an earnest attempt at repairs was made only after the initial cataloguing and photography were completed in March of 1966. The job of matching additional heads to torsos was the most difficult, as the necks of most of the loose heads had become so abraded after having been severed for so long that only 23 more heads were successfully matched with torsos. Countless fragments of heads, limbs, and torsos were matched and re-joined, however. The easiest job because of the size of its parts, but the most spectacular, was the reconstruction of HT 58, pictured here in the condition in which we found it, and with the Plates in its reconstructed form.

The medium used in effecting repairs was a brand of epoxy resin, Araldite AY 103 and Hardener HY 456, manufactured by CIBA of Basel, and recommended by the manufacturers for the repair of soapstone. After matched objects had been repaired, several unidentifiable fragments of stone selected visually for varying ranges of colour were pulverized and mixed with the epoxy; this compound was used to fill cracks and re-sculpt some abraded features. During the final stage of hardening of the mixture, the re-sculpted parts were dusted with pulverized stone of a colour similar to that of the image, and in most cases the repaired areas are barely visible.

Categories of Images

The Plates are divided into five categories: Complete Figures (Head and Torso, designated HT); Repaired Figures (bearing the combined numbers of the original fragments); Heads (designated H); Torsos (designated T); and Selected Miscellaneous Objects. All the complete figures, 289 in number, and all the figures whose heads were later re-joined, 23 in number, are represented. Most are shown in front and side views. In some cases rear views and details are shown; and a few are represented in one photograph only. Most of the heads are represented in front and side views; in some cases, because of the fragmentary or abraded state of the object, one view suffices. Several of the poorer heads and head fragments are not pictured; these are listed in the introduction to the Heads section. In the original numbering, 801 Torsos, excluding the countless severed bases of stools, were designated. No attempt was made to classify these. 157 of them are represented in the Plates, selected arbitrarily for their quality and interest; most were photographed only once. The final category, Selected Miscellaneous Objects, includes various articles held by or found in association with the other stones.

HT 58, before repairs.

The Captions

As mentioned previously, and in the Preface to this book (p. x), a great amount of data was obtained and recorded, with a view toward conducting a computer-based correlational analysis. We carefully recorded measurements and elaborate descriptions of hairstyles, headgear, jewellery, dress, body scarification, weaponry and other accoutrements, and stool types. We also recorded the weights of the complete and repaired figures. The aim here, however, is the visual representation of the images themselves; over-long captions would necessitate reduction in the size of the plates. Therefore, the captions have been kept as brief as possible, including only descriptions of such features as are not readily apparent in the photographs. The rest of the data will be retained in the event that a statistical analysis becomes feasible — and is deemed potentially fruitful.

To keep the captions at once as brief and as comprehensive as possible, the following abbreviations and designations have been adopted:

r.h. — right hand
l.h. — left hand
cic. — cicatrization
frag. — fragment
r.v.c. — raised vertical cicatrice
unident. obj. — unidentified object

"calabash-bottle motif" refers to the representations of tiny calabashes on the heads and arms of several of the figures. Similar containers are in widespread use as personal accoutrements in the Sudanic areas of Africa; they generally hold herbal medicines and are worn as protective charms.

"floral motif" refers to a small 4-sided decoration, much like the petals of a flower, seen on several caps.

"bell motif" is a designation for a sometimes bell-shaped, sometimes triangular, decoration on some caps.

"incised line down spine," or "incised spine," are designations applied to those images whose spinal columns are represented by incised lines, in the manner of the Modakẹkẹ image pictured in figs. V.7,8 (p. 56).

Other significant features which are not apparent from the photographs are described in full.

Complete figures
(Head and torso)

The "King of the Images." 59 kg., 87 cm.

The King, side.

1
2

HT 1. 38 kg., 64 cm.

HT 1, side.

3

HT 2. R.h. held staff. 51 kg., 76 cm.

HT 2, side.

5

6

HT 3. 25 kg.,
54 cm.

HT 3, side.

7

8

HT 4. 30 kg.,
64 cm.

HT 4, side.

9

10

HT 5-6

11

HT 5. Beard on chin. 33 kg., 71 cm.

HT 5, side.

12

HT 6. 22 kg., 57 cm.

13

HT 6, side.

14

HT 7. 4 rows cic.
down back.
12 kg., 47 cm.

15

HT 7, side.

16

HT 7, detail,
showing facial
scarification.

17

HT 8-9

18

HT 8, side.

19

HT 8. Necklace tie like HT 127. Small calabash-bottle motif on cap. R.h. held staff. 26 kg., 64 cm.

20

HT 9, side.

21

HT 9. Calabash-bottle motif on cap. 14 kg., 44 cm.

HT 10.
Calabash-bottle
and floral motifs
on cap. 4 r.v.c.
back of neck.
15 kg., 51 cm.

HT 10, side.

22

23

HT 11. Dagger l.
hip. 20 kg.,
50 cm.

HT 11, side.

24

25

HT 12-13

26

HT 12. Single bottle-like decor on cap. L.h. holds staff. 17 kg., 50 cm.

HT 12, side.

27

28

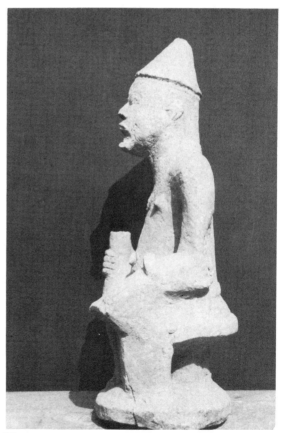

HT 13. 3 r.v.c. back of neck. 39 kg., 68 cm.

HT 13, side.

29

HT 14. 3 r.v.c.
back of neck.
32 kg., 73 cm.

HT 14, side.

30

31

HT 15. 29 kg.,
72 cm.

HT 15, side.

32

33

HT 16-17

HT 16. R.h. held fly whisk over r. shoulder. Bare buttocks, like HT 28. 26 kg., 58 cm.

34

HT 16, side.

35

HT 17. 60 cm.

36

HT 17, side.

37

HT 18. R.h. held staff or bow. Small quiver on back. Incised line down spine. 38 kg., 61 cm.

HT 18, side.

38

39

HT 19. L.h. held staff. Dagger under l. arm. 39 kg., 69 cm.

HT 19, side.

40

41

HT 20-21

42

HT 20. Incised line down spine. 32 kg., 62 cm.

HT 20, side.

43

44

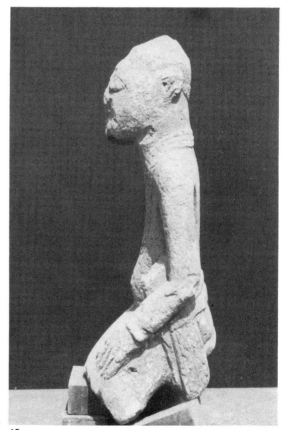

HT 21. Unident. obj. (sheathed dagger?) under l. arm. 19 kg., 58 cm.

HT 21, side.

45

HT 22. Matched
with T 280.
51 kg., 56 cm.

46

HT 23. 14 kg.,
50 cm.

47

HT 24. 57 cm.

48

HT 24, side.

49

HT 25-26

HT 25. L.h. held
staff. 30 kg.,
63 cm.

50

HT 26. 17 kg.,
56 cm.

51

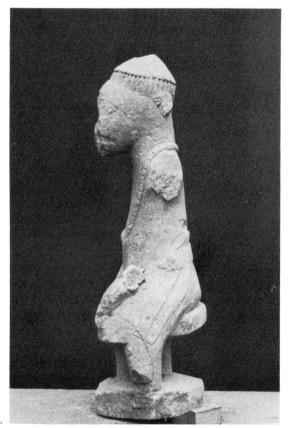

HT 26, side.

52

HT 27. 26 kg.,
62 cm.

53

HT 27, side.

54

HT 28

55

HT 28. 41 kg.,
74 cm.

HT 28, side.

56

HT 28, back.

57

HT 29. 4 r.v.c.
back of neck.
22 kg., 65 cm.

HT 29, side.

58

59

HT 30. R.h. held
staff. 22 kg.,
55 cm.

HT 30, side.

60

61

HT 31. 21 kg., 53 cm.

HT 31, side.

62

63

HT 32. Two rows herringbone cic. down back (cf. HT 77). 39 kg., 76 cm.

HT 32, side.

64

65

HT 33. 3 r.v.c.
back of neck.
50 kg., 74 cm.

66

HT 33, r. side.

67

HT 33, l. side.

68

HT 34-35

HT 34.
Calabash-bottle
motif on cap. R.h.
held staff. 47 kg.,
78 cm.

HT 34, side.

69   70

HT 35. Matched
with T 791.
3 r.v.c. back of
neck. Dagger
l. hip. 32 kg.,
66 cm.

HT 35, side.

71   72

73

HT 36.
Calabash-bottle
motif on cap.
17 kg., 51 cm.

HT 36, side.

74

75

HT 37.
Calabash-bottle
motif on cap.
24 kg., 60 cm.

HT 37, side.

76

HT 38-39

77

HT 38. L.h. held staff. 39 kg., 66 cm.

HT 38, side.

78

79

HT 39. 3 r.v.c. back of neck. Two rows herringbone cic. down back (cf. HT 127). Dagger l. hip. 35 kg., 66 cm.

HT 39, side.

80

HT 40.
Cross-hatched
cic. down back.
31 kg., 70 cm.

81

HT 40, side.

82

HT 41.
Calabash-bottle
motif front of
cap, bell motif
rear. Dagger
l. hip. 33 kg.,
69 cm.

83

HT 41, side.

84

85

HT 42. 4-sided cap. Necklace tie like HT 108. 32 kg., 67 cm.

HT 42, side.

86

87

HT 43. 4-sided cap. 3 r.v.c. back of neck. 21 kg., 57 cm.

HT 43, side.

88

HT 44. 4-sided
cap. L.h. held
bow. 44 kg.,
66 cm.

89

HT 44, side.

90

HT 45. 4-sided
cap, calabash-
bottle motif front.
R.h. held staff.
32 kg., 70 cm.

91

HT 45, side.

92

HT 46-47

93

HT 46, side.

94

HT 46. 4-sided cap. 3 r.v.c. back of neck. Necklace tie like HT 217. Dagger l. hip. 19 kg., 50 cm.

HT 47. 5-sided cap. 14 kg., 50 cm.

95

HT 47, side.

96

97

98

HT 48. 6-sided cap. Stool base filled with epoxy compound. 9 kg., 50 cm.

HT 48, side.

99

100

HT 49. 11-sided cap. 15 kg., 57 cm.

HT 49, side.

HT 50-51

101

HT 50. 11-ridged
cap. 16 kg.,
58 cm.

HT 50, side.

102

HT 51. 3 r.v.c.
back of neck.
Dagger l. hip.
25 kg., 69 cm.

103

HT 51, side.

104

HT 52. 21 kg.,
48 cm.

HT 52, side.

105

106

HT 53. 14 kg.,
47 cm.

107

HT 53, side.

108

HT 54-55

109

HT 54. Necklace
tie like HT 67.
14 kg., 49 cm.

HT 54, side.

110

HT 55. Possibly
no feet were
carved. 22 kg.,
53 cm.

111

HT 55, side.

112

HT 56. Possibly no feet were carved. 18 kg., 50 cm.

113

HT 56, side.

114

HT 57. Hands apparently held staff. 16 kg., 48 cm.

115

HT 57, side.

116

HT 58-59

117

HT 58, side.

118

HT 58. *"Tapa"* (Nupe) figure. The largest in the collection. 104 kg., 110 cm.

HT 59. 3 r.v.c. back of neck. 18 kg., 56 cm.

119

HT 59, side.

120

HT 60. Female.
26 kg., 55 cm.

121

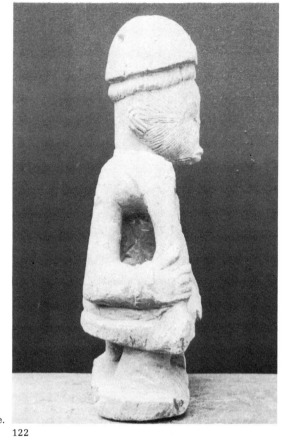

HT 60, side.

122

HT 61. 14 kg.,
47 cm.

123

HT 61, side.

124

HT 62-63

125

HT 62. Back of
head is H 79.
3 r.v.c. back of
neck. 32 kg.,
69 cm.

HT 62, side.

126

127

HT 63. Necklace
tie like HT 108.
Dagger l. hip.
50 kg., 82 cm.

HT 63, side.

128

134

HT 64. 12 kg., 38 cm.

HT 64, side.

129

130

HT 65. Quiver opens to l. shoulder. L.h. holds bow. 35 kg., 64 cm.

HT 65, side.

131

132

HT 66

133

HT 66. Female.
R.h. held cutlass
over r. shoulder.
12 kg., 46 cm.

HT 66, side.

134

HT 67. L.h. held
bow. Large
dagger behind.
52 kg., 77 cm.

135

HT 67, side.

136

HT 67, back.

137

HT 68-69

138

HT 68. 3 r.v.c.
back of neck. L.h.
held staff. 31 kg.,
64 cm.

HT 68, side.

139

HT 69. Two
striations angling
away from lower
lip. Short sash
over r. shoulder.
24 kg., 55 cm.

140

HT 69, side.

141

HT 70.
Calabash-bottle
motif top of cap.
3 r.v.c. back of
neck. Dagger
l. hip. L.h. held
bow. 26 kg.,
57 cm.

142

HT 70, side.

143

HT 71.
Calabash-bottle
motif front of
cap. 4 r.v.c. back
of neck. 18 kg.,
50 cm.

144

HT 71, side.

145

HT 72. 14 kg., 48 cm.

HT 72, side.

146

147

HT 73. 26 kg., 61 cm.

HT 73, side.

148

149

HT 74. 3 r.v.c.
back of neck.
Dagger l. side. 44
kg., 70 cm.

HT 74, side.

150

151

HT 75. 35 kg.,
76 cm.

HT 75, side.

152

153

HT 76

HT 76. 33 kg., 64 cm.

154

HT 76, side.

155

HT 77. Peculiar
nub at l. temple.
Teardrop motif
on cap. Dagger
l. hip. Beard
filled with epoxy
compound.
45 kg., 80 cm.

156

HT 77, side.

157

HT 77, back.

158

159

HT 78. 3 r.v.c.
back of neck.
Necklace tie like
HT 77. 73 kg.,
90 cm.

HT 78, side.

160

161

HT 79. 3 r.v.c.
back of neck. L.h.
held staff. Full
beard. 31 kg.,
61 cm.

HT 79, side.

162

HT 80. Female. 3 r.v.c. back of neck. R.h. held cutlass to r. shoulder. 30 kg., 58 cm.

163

HT 80, side.

164

HT 81. 3 r.v.c. back of neck. Quiver opens to l. shoulder. L.h. holds small bow on lap. 33 kg., 65 cm.

165

HT 81, side.

166

HT 82-83

167

HT 82. 3 r.v.c.
back of neck. R.h.
held staff. 17 kg.,
54 cm.

HT 82, side.

168

169

HT 83. Dagger
l. hip, bow l.h.
28 kg., 59 cm.

HT 83, side.

170

HT 84. Necklace tie like HT 189. 30 kg., 64 cm.

171

HT 84, side.

172

HT 85. 8 kg., 39 cm.

173

HT 86-87

174

HT 86. Incised
line down spine.
R.h. held object
to r. shoulder.
26 kg., 62 cm.

HT 86, side.

175

HT 87. Incised
line down spine.
R.h. held object
to r. shoulder.
26 kg., 62 cm.

176

HT 87, side.

177

HT 88. Incised
line down spine.
17 kg., 52 cm.

178

HT 89. Female.
Necklace tie: 2
tassels set apart,
hanging straight
down. Cic. on
back like HT 77,
but herringbone
motif reversed.
R.h. held cutlass
to r. shoulder.
20 kg., 51 cm.

HT 89, side.

179

180

181

HT 90. Female.
R.h. holds cutlass
to r. shoulder.
18 kg., 55 cm.

HT 90, side.

182

HT 91. Female.
10 kg., 45 cm.

183

HT 91, side.

184

185

HT 92. Necklace tie like HT 189. 14 kg., 44 cm.

HT 92, side.

186

HT 93. Female. Incised line down spine. 16 kg., 50 cm.

187

151

HT 94. Female.
R.h. held cutlass
to r. shoulder.
20 kg., 52 cm.

188

HT 94, side.

189

HT 95. Probably
female (l. breast
broken off). R.h.
held cutlass to r.
shoulder. 13 kg.,
47 cm.

190

HT 95, side.

191

HT 96. Female. 3 r.v.c. back of neck. Cic. on back like HT 77, but herringbone motif reversed. R.h. held cutlass over r. shoulder. 12 kg., 42 cm.

HT 96, side.

192

193

HT 97. Female. R.h. held cutlass to r. shoulder. 20 kg., 46 cm.

HT 97, side.

194

195

196

HT 98. Female. L.h. fingers not carved. 23 kg., 74 cm.

HT 98, side.

197

198

HT 99. Female. L.h. to l. breast. 17 kg., 54 cm.

HT 99, side.

199

HT 100. Female.
33 kg., 74 cm.

HT 100, side.

200

201

HT 101. Female.
L.h. held cutlass,
point down to
l. foot. 18 kg.,
54 cm.

HT 101, side.

202

203

HT 102-103

204

HT 102. Female.
R.h. held cutlass
to r. shoulder.
29 kg., 60 cm.

HT 102, side.

205

206

HT 103. Female.
Incised spine.
34 kg., 74 cm.

HT 104. 25 kg.,
59 cm.

HT 104, side.

207

208

HT 105. 3 r.v.c.
back of neck.
Necklace tie like
HT 89. L.h. held
bow. 36 kg.,
62 cm.

209

HT 105, side.

210

211

HT 106. Female.
18 kg., 54 cm.

HT 106, side.

212

213

HT 107. Female.
32 kg., 67 cm.

HT 107, side.

214

215

HT 108. Female.
R.h. holds cutlass
on lap, blade
held by l.h.
59 kg., 61 cm.

HT 108, side.
216

HT 108, back.
217

HT 109-110

218

HT 109. Female.
45 kg., 76 cm.

HT 109, side.

219

HT 110. L.h. held
staff, or bow
(although figure
has no quiver).
Dagger l. hip.
36 kg., 68 cm.

220

HT 110, side.

221

HT 111. 12 kg., 48 cm.

222

HT 111, side.

223

HT 112. L.h. held unident. obj. (possibly bow) down to l. knee. 31 kg., 57 cm.

224

HT 112, side.

225

HT 113-114

226

227

HT 113. Female.
25 kg., 52 cm.

HT 113, side.

228

229

HT 114. 16 kg.,
49 cm.

HT 114, side.

HT 115. 3 r.v.c.
back of neck.
Necklace tie like
HT 108. Long
beard down
chest. Calabash-
bottle l. arm.
R.h. held staff.
45 kg., 78 cm.

HT 115, side.

230

231

HT 115, back.

232

HT 116. 43 cm.

233

HT 117-118

234

HT 117. Single row herringbone cic. down back. L.h. holds dagger, point down. 47 cm.

HT 117, side.

235

HT 118. 22 kg., 57 cm.

236

HT 118, side.

237

HT 119. Necklace tie like HT 193. Quiver on back, but no strap across chest. 25 kg., 60 cm.

238

HT 119, side.

239

240

HT 120. Female. 3 r.v.c. back of neck. Necklace tie like HT 108. Cic. on back like HT 77 and HT 170. 35 kg., 64 cm.

HT 120, side.

241

HT 121-122

HT 121. 50 cm.

242

HT 122. 3 r.v.c.
back of neck.
31 kg., 63 cm.

243

HT 122, side.

244

HT 123. Female. Dagger l. hip (an unusual female accoutrement). 3 r.v.c. back of neck. Necklace tie like HT 108. 5 rows herringbone cic. down back, sim. to HT 127. 57 kg., 66 cm.

HT 123, side.

245

246

HT 124. 3 r.v.c. back of neck. Cic. on back like HT 89. 28 kg., 57 cm.

HT 124, side.

247

248

249

HT 125.
Calabash-bottle
motif top of head.
Dagger l. hip.
57 cm.

HT 125, side.

250

251

HT 126. 20 kg.,
55 cm.

HT 126, side.

252

HT 127. Female.
Pregnant? 22 kg.,
54 cm.

253

HT 127, side.

254

HT 127, back.

255

HT 128

HT 128. 23 kg.,
59 cm.

256

HT 128, side.

257

HT 128, back.

258

170

259

HT 129, side.

260

HT 129. Female. R.h. held cutlass over r. shoulder. 40 kg., 71 cm.

HT 130. Necklace tie sim. to HT 177. Calabash-bottle motif l. arm. 33 kg., 65 cm.

261

HT 130, side.

262

HT 131

263

HT 131. Necklace tie like HT 108. 4 rows raised bead-like cicatrices down back. Hands probably held staff, which stood directly in front. 59 cm.

HT 131, side.

264

HT 132. Female.
34 kg., 68 cm.

265

HT 132, side.

266

HT 132, back.

267

268

HT 133. Female.
3 r.v.c. back of
neck. Necklace
tie like HT 127.
4 rows reversed
herringbone cic.
down back, like
HT 89. 28 kg.,
56 cm.

HT 133, side.

269

HT 134. Female.
R.h. held cutlass
to r. shoulder.
21 kg., 60 cm.

270

HT 134, side.

271

272

HT 135. Female.
Incised spine.
21 kg., 57 cm.

HT 135, side.

273

HT 136. 3 r.v.c.
back of neck. L.h.
holds bow.
25 kg., 58 cm.

274

HT 136, side.

275

HT 137

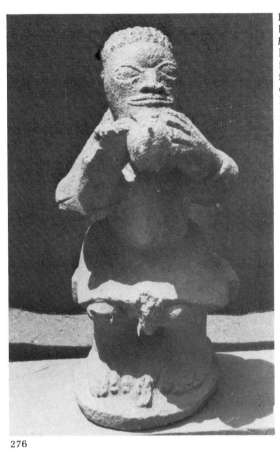

HT 137. Called by Esiẹ people Elérù èrè, "the load-bearing image." A beard flows over the object held in the hands, which is most likely the head of a staff which extended down in front of the image; the figure is resting its chin upon it. 50 kg., 61 cm.

276

HT 137, side.

277

HT 137, back.

278

HT 138. Female.
Necklace tie like
HT 108. 21 kg.,
51 cm.

HT 138, side.

279

280

HT 139. Necklace
tie sim. to HT
127. Dagger l.
hip. 19 kg.,
53 cm.

HT 139, side.

281

282

HT 141-142

283

HT 141. (Due to a numbering error, there is no HT 140.) Female. 10 kg., 38 cm.

HT 141, side.

284

285

HT 142. Female. 3 r.v.c. back of neck. Necklace tie sim. to HT 67. 19 kg., 53 cm.

HT 142, side.

286

HT 143. Necklace
tie sim. to HT 77.
28 kg., 61 cm.

HT 143, side.

287

288

HT 144. Female.
3 r.v.c. back of
neck. 4 rows
reversed
herringbone cic.
down back, like
HT 89. 24 kg.,
64 cm.

HT 144, side.

289

290

HT 145-146

HT 145. Female.
Sash over
l. shoulder.
Dagger l. hip (an
unusual female
accoutrement).
53 cm.

291

HT 145, side.

292

HT 146. Incised
spine. 29 kg.,
57 cm.

293

HT 147. Female. Necklace tie like HT 189. 39 kg., 61 cm.

294

HT 147, side.

295

HT 148. Necklace tie like HT 108. Quiver, but no strap. L.h. held bow. 15 kg., 53 cm.

296

HT 148, side.

297

HT 149-150

298

HT 149. 52 cm.

HT 149, side.

299

300

HT 150. 25 kg., 66 cm.

HT 150, side.

301

182

HT 151. 3 r.v.c.
back of neck.
Necklace tie like
HT 127. 42 kg.,
68 cm.

302

HT 151, side.

303

HT 152. Female.
3 r.v.c. back of
neck. L.h. holds
unident. obj.
40 kg., 71 cm.

304

HT 152, side.

305

HT 153-154

306

HT 153. Female.
R.h. held cutlass
to r. shoulder.
29 kg., 53 cm.

HT 153, side.

307

308

HT 154. 18 kg.,
50 cm.

HT 154, side.

309

HT 155. Necklace
tie like HT 67.
29 kg., 67 cm.

310

HT 155, side.

311

HT 156. Female
3 r.v.c. back of
neck. R.h. held
cutlass to r.
shoulder. 52 kg.,
54 cm.

312

HT 156, side.

313

HT 157-158

314

HT 157, side.

315

HT 157. Matched with T 78. Necklace tie like HT 67. 51 kg., 57 cm.

HT 158. Necklace tie like HT 67. 16 kg., 52 cm.

316

HT 158, side.

317

186

HT 159. Necklace
tie like HT 67.
Dagger l. hip.
Hands probably
held staff, centre.
33 kg., 57 cm.

318

HT 159, side.

319

HT 160. Necklace
tie like HT 67.
Dagger l. hip.
Hands probably
held staff, centre.
21 kg., 59 cm.

320

HT 160, side.

321

HT 161-162

322

HT 161. Necklace tie like HT 67. R.h. probably held staff. 26 kg., 58 cm.

HT 161, side.

323

324

HT 162. 3 r.v.c. back of neck. Necklace tie like HT 108. 87 kg., 73 cm.

HT 162, side.

325

HT 163. Female.
R.h. held cutlass
to r. shoulder.
19 kg., 59 cm.

326

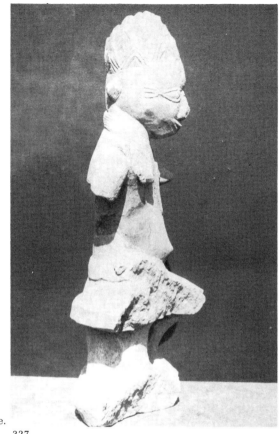

HT 163, side.

327

328

HT 164. 25 kg.,
59 cm.

HT 164, side.

329

HT 165-166

330

HT 165. L.h. held
bow. 18 kg.,
57 cm.

HT 165, side.

331

HT 166. Quiver
straight up back.
17 kg., 54 cm.

332

HT 166, side.

333

HT 167. 14 kg., 49 cm.

334

HT 168. Female. 9 kg., 47 cm.

335

HT 168, side.

336

HT 169. Necklace tie like HT 127. 25 kg., 65 cm.

337

HT 170

338

HT 170. 34 kg.,
71 cm.

HT 170, side.

339

HT 170, back.

340

HT 171. 3 r.v.c.
back of neck.
27 kg., 61 cm.

341

HT 171, side.

342

HT 172. 13 kg.,
43 cm.

343

HT 172, side.

344

HT 173. Calabash-bottle motif on forehead. Necklace tie like HT 189. 12 kg., 43 cm.

345

HT 173, side.

346

HT 174. 3 r.v.c. back of neck. R.h. holds cutlass across lap, point under l.h. 17 kg., 49 cm.

347

HT 174, side.

348

HT 175. L.h. held
bow. 18 kg.,
54 cm.

HT 175, side.

349

350

HT 176. Female.
R.h. held cutlass
to r. shoulder.
25 kg., 62 cm.

HT 176, side.

351

352

HT 177

353

HT 177. Female.
108 kg., 71 cm.

HT 177, side.

354

HT 177, back.

355

HT 178. Female. 3 r.v.c. back of neck. R.h. held cutlass over r. shoulder. 21 kg., 52 cm.

HT 178, side.

356

357

HT 179. 3 r.v.c. back of neck. 22 kg., 57 cm.

HT 179, side.

358

359

HT 180

360

HT 180. 3 r.v.c.
back of neck.
Necklace tie like
HT 127. R.h.
holds fly whisk
down r. leg.
30 kg., 70 cm.

HT 180, side.

361

198

HT 181. Female.
55 kg., 54 cm.

362

HT 181, side.

363

HT 181, back.

364

HT 182-183

365

HT 182. 24 kg., 52 cm.

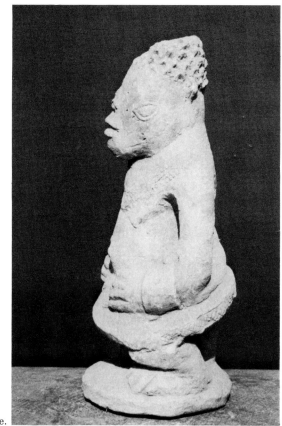

HT 182, side.

366

HT 183. Female? R.h. holds cutlass to r. shoulder. 24 kg., 55 cm.

367

HT 183, side.

368

HT 184. Female.
19 kg., 51 cm.

369

HT 184, side.

370

HT 185. Female.
R.h. held cutlass
over r. shoulder.
17 kg., 47 cm.

371

HT 185, side.

372

HT 186-187

373

HT 186. R.h. holds top of quiver, over r. shoulder. L.h. held bow. 24 kg., 58 cm.

HT 186, side.

374

375

HT 187. Tips of arrows show in quiver. L.h. held bow. 24 kg., 58 cm.

HT 187, side.

376

HT 188. A blacksmith? 3 r.v.c. back of neck. Herringbone cic. on back, like HT 170. 2 calabash-bottles 1. arm. R.h. holds hammer, L.h. holds flat object. 21 kg., 60 cm.

377

HT 188, side.

378

HT 188, detail, showing tools held on lap.

379

HT 189

HT 189. 16 kg., 53 cm.

380

HT 189, side.

381

HT 189, back.

382

HT 190. Female.
43 kg., 66 cm.

383

HT 190, side.
384

HT 190, back.
385

HT 191-192

HT 191. 41 cm.

386

HT 191, side.

387

388

HT 192. R.h. held
staff. Calabash-
bottle motif
top of head.
20 kg., 53 cm.

HT 192, side.

389

HT 193. Female.
43 kg., 61 cm.

390

HT 193, side.
391

HT 193, back.
392

HT 194. Female?
4 r.v.c. back of
neck. Cic. on
back like HT 193.
R.h. held cutlass,
point down.
22 kg., 55 cm.

393

HT 194, side.

394

HT 195. Standing
figure. Incised
spine. 17 kg.,
49 cm.

395

HT 195, side.

396

HT 196. 3 r.v.c. back of neck. Necklace tie like HT 127. 30 kg., 60 cm.

397

HT 196, side.

398

HT 197. 4 r.v.c. back of neck. R.h. held staff, down r. leg. 33 kg., 64 cm.

399

HT 197, side.

400

HT 198-199

401

HT 198. Female?
L.h. held staff.
15 kg., 47 cm.

HT 198, side.

402

403

HT 199. Female.
3 r.v.c. back of
neck. R.h. held
cutlass, point to
r. shoulder.
15 kg., 47 cm.

HT 199, side.

404

405

406

HT 200. Standing figure, like HT 195. 20 kg., 53 cm.

HT 200, side.

HT 201. 22 kg., 51 cm.

407

408

HT 201, side.

409

HT 202. Female?
R.h. held cutlass
over r. shoulder.
27 kg., 60 cm.

HT 202, side.

410

411

HT 203. R.h. held
staff to top of r.
foot. 26 kg.,
63 cm.

HT 203, side.

412

HT 204. 17 kg.,
54 cm.

413

HT 204, side.

414

HT 205

HT 205. Female.
Cic. on back like
HT 132. 15 kg.,
47 cm.

415

HT 205, side.

416

HT 205, back.

417

HT 206. Necklace tie like HT 67. 25 kg., 58 cm.

418

HT 206, side.

419

HT 207. Female. 14 kg., 49 cm.

420

HT 207, side.

421

HT 208-209

422

HT 208. 3 r.v.c.
back of neck.
Decorated quiver.
Dagger l. hip.
17 kg., 50 cm.

HT 208, side.

423

HT 209. 16 kg.,
47 cm.

424

HT 209, side.

425

426

HT 210.
Decorated quiver.
20 kg., 50 cm.

HT 210, side.

427

428

HT 211. L.h. held
bow. 23 kg.,
61 cm.

HT 211, side.

429

HT 212-213

430

HT 212. Female.
R.h. holds cutlass
over r. shoulder.
20 kg., 56 cm.

HT 212, side.

431

432

HT 213. Female.
R.h. held cutlass
to r. shoulder.
32 kg., 62 cm.

HT 213, side.

433

HT 214. Female.
R.h. held cutlass
over r. shoulder.
14 kg., 47 cm.

HT 214, side.

434

435

HT 215. Female.
R.h. held cutlass,
point down.
74 kg., 66 cm.

436

HT 215, side.

437

HT 216

HT 216. Female.
4 r.v.c. back of
neck. R.h. holds
cutlass on lap.
34 kg., 61 cm.

HT 216, side.

438

439

HT 217. 77 cm.

440

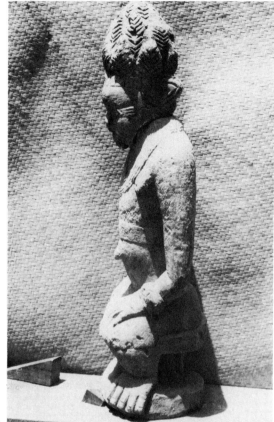

HT 217, side.

441

HT 217, back.

442

HT 218. 3 r.v.c. back of neck. Dagger l. side. 22 kg., 58 cm.

HT 218, side.

443

444

HT 219. Dagger on back. 25 kg., 58 cm.

HT 219, back.

445

446

HT 220. Female?
Cutlass point at r.
shoulder. 28 kg.,
68 cm.

HT 220, side.

447

448

HT 221. Female.
12 kg., 47 cm.

HT 221, side.

449

450

HT 222. Female.
17 kg., 51 cm.

451

HT 223. Incised
spine. R.h. held
staff. 14 kg.,
36 cm.

452

HT 223, side.

453

HT 224. Female.
27 kg., 58 cm.

454

HT 224, side.

455

HT 225. Female.
R.h. holds cutlass
over r. shoulder.
40 kg., 60 cm.

456

HT 225, side.

457

HT 226

458

HT 226. Dagger
l. rear. Bare
buttocks. Peculiar
tasseled
ornament back of
head. 34 kg.,
73 cm.

HT 226, side.

459

HT 226, back.

460

HT 227. Female.
Necklace tie like
HT 127. 14 kg.,
40 cm.

HT 227, side.

461

462

HT 228. Matched
with T 704.
Necklace tie like
HT 181. Shoulder
blades delineated
by incised lines.
59 kg., 57 cm.

HT 228, side.

463

464

HT 229-230

HT 229. No measurement.

465

HT 230. 3 r.v.c. back of neck. Necklace tie like HT 108. 34 kg., 71 cm.

466

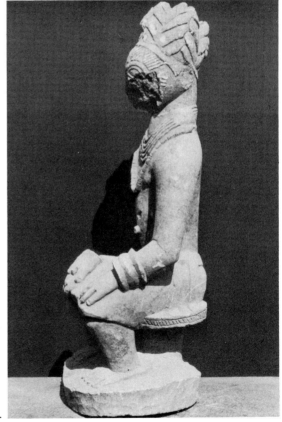

HT 230, side.

467

HT 231. Female.
43 cm.

HT 231, side.

468

469

HT 232. Female.
R.h. held cutlass
to r. shoulder.
23 kg., 52 cm.

470

HT 232, side.

471

HT 233-234

472

HT 233. Holding
shield. 33 kg.,
61 cm.

HT 233, side.

473

474

HT 234. L.h. held
bow. 21 kg.,
55 cm.

HT 234, side.

475

HT 235. Quiver, but no strap. 12 kg., 45 cm.

HT 235, side.

476

477

HT 236. 3 r.v.c. back of neck. L.h. holds sheathed dagger. 22 kg., 69 cm.

HT 236, side.

478

479

HT 237-238

480

HT 237. 4 r.v.c.
back of neck. L.h.
held dagger.
17 kg., 51 cm.

HT 237, side.

481

482

HT 238. Female.
3 r.v.c. back of
neck. 14 kg.,
50 cm.

HT 238, side.

483

HT 239. R.h. probably held staff. 38 kg., 69 cm.

484

HT 239, side.

485

HT 240. 25 kg., 63 cm.

486

HT 240, side.

487

HT 241-242

HT 241. 3 r.v.c. back of neck. Necklace tie like HT 67. Arrows show in quiver. 20 kg., 51 cm.

488

HT 241, side.

489

HT 242. 3 r.v.c. back of neck. Necklace tie like HT 285. 13 kg., 43 cm.

490

491

HT 243. R.h. probably held staff. 18 kg., 50 cm.

HT 243, side.

492

493

HT 244. Small cap top of head. 60 cm.

HT 244, side.

494

Ht 245. Female.
Necklace tie like
HT 108. 16 kg.,
47 cm.

HT 245, side.

495

496

HT 246. Female.
3 r.v.c. back of
neck. Tiny legs
and feet. 14 kg.,
47 cm.

HT 246, side.

497

498

HT 247. 14 kg.,
48 cm.

HT 247, side.

499

500

HT 248. 3 r.v.c.
back of neck. L.h.
holds bow.
11 kg., 48 cm.

HT 248, side.

501

502

503

HT 249. R.h. held staff. 21 kg., 51 cm.

HT 249, side.

504

505

HT 250. Cic. on back like HT 77. L.h. held staff. 20 kg., 50 cm.

HT 250, side.

506

507

HT 251. 3 r.v.c.
back of neck. L.h.
held bow. Small
dagger l. hip.
18 kg., 55 cm.

HT 251, side.

508

HT 252. Cic. on
back like HT 89.
47 cm.

509

HT 252, side.

510

511

HT 253. L.h. held
bow. 16 kg.,
48 cm.

HT 253, side.

512

513

HT 254. Female?
R.h. holds cutlass
to r. shoulder.
12 kg., 38 cm.

HT 254, side.

514

515

HT 255.
Calabash-bottle
motif top of head.
L.h. held bow.
31 kg., 64 cm.

HT 255, side.

516

HT 256. L.h.
holds bow.
36 kg., 65 cm.

517

HT 256, side.

518

HT 257-258

519

HT 257. 3 r.v.c.
back of neck.
27 kg., 65 cm.

HT 257, side.

520

521

HT 258. Female.
27 kg., 65 cm.

HT 258, side.

522

242

HT 259. Base of
stool and r. leg
filled with some
compound prior
to 1965. 70 cm.

523

HT 259, side.

524

HT 260. 35 kg.,
67 cm.

525

HT 260, side.

526

HT 261-262

527

HT 261. 12 kg., 43 cm.

HT 261, side.

528

529

HT 262. Feet on edge of stool top. 9 kg., 35 cm.

HT 262, side.

530

531

HT 263. Narrow quiver, but no strap. 25 kg., 57 cm.

HT 263, side.

532

533

HT 264. Incised spine. 17 kg., 50 cm.

HT 264, side.

534

535

HT 265. Dagger, broken, l. hip. 26 kg., 61 cm.

HT 265, side.

536

537

HT 266. Arrow tips show in quiver. 17 kg., 51 cm.

HT 266, side.

538

HT 267. Female.
3 r.v.c. back of
neck. Necklace
tie like HT 181.
13 kg., 40 cm.

HT 267, side.

539

540

HT 268

541

HT 268. Not evident what this figure is doing. 3 r.v.c. back of neck. Necklace tie like HT 108. Large braid from top of head down r. side. 19 kg., 51 cm.

HT 268, l. side.

542

HT 268, r. side.

543

HT 269. Female. Incised spine. Sides of head shaved, strip of hair down middle. 14 kg., 44 cm.

544

HT 269, side.

545

HT 270. Female. *Ìlàrí* figure (cf. pp. 58-9, 67-8). Cic. on back like HT 205. R. side of head shaved. Designated as an attendant to the "King." 40 kg., 55 cm.

546

HT 270, side.

547

548

HT 271. Female. *Ìlàrí* figure. L. side of head shaved. 5 kg., 31 cm.

HT 271, side

549

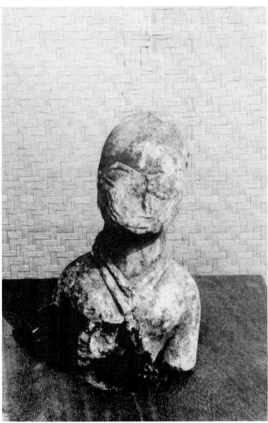

550

HT 272. Female? *Ìlàrí* figure. R. side of head shaved. No measurement.

HT 272, side.

551

HT 273. Female, *Ìlarì* figure, r. side of head shaved. Kneeling, naked, holding open pod of kola nuts. Stolen from collection in April, 1974. 33 cm.

HT 273, side.

552

553

HT 274. Female, naked, kneeling. Incised spine. 29 cm.

HT 274, side.

554

555

HT 275-276

556

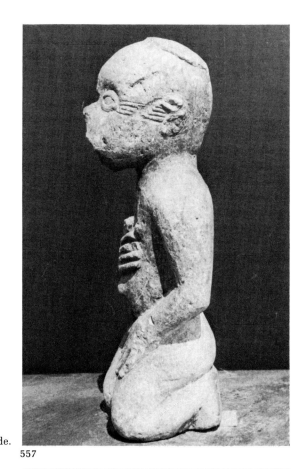

HT 275. Naked, kneeling. Head shaved but for a circular topknot. 10 kg., 40 cm.

HT 275, side.

557

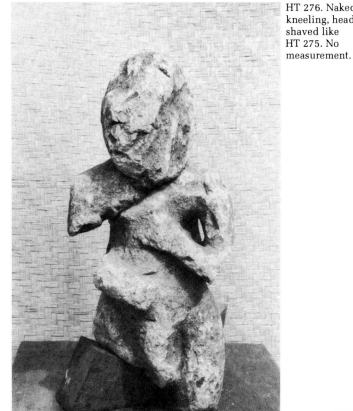

558

HT 276. Naked, kneeling, head shaved like HT 275. No measurement.

HT 276, side.

559

HT 277. 8 kg.,
39 cm.

560

HT 277, side.

561

HT 278. Female.
Incised spine.
R.h. held staff.
Small dagger
l. side. 25 kg.,
60 cm.

562

HT 278, side.

563

HT 279-280

HT 279. Stool covered by skirt. R. hand on r. cheek. 15 kg., 42 cm.

564

HT 279, side.

565

HT 280. No measurement.

566

HT 280, side.

567

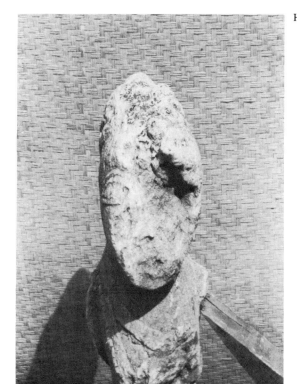

HT 281. 45 cm.

568

HT 281, side.

569

HT 282. Female.
3 r.v.c. back of
neck. 23 kg.,
61 cm.

570

HT 283-284

571

HT 283, side.

572

HT 283. Female. Cutlass point at r. shoulder. 11 kg., 50 cm.

573

HT 284. Narrow quiver, but no strap. Incised spine. 20 kg., 52 cm.

HT 285. Female.
R.h. held cutlass
to r. shoulder.
40 kg., 55 cm.

574

HT 285, side.

575

HT 285, back.

576

HT 286-287

577

HT 286. 8 kg., 37 cm.

HT 286, side.

578

579

HT 287. Female. R.h. holds cutlass over r. shoulder. 17 kg., 40 cm.

HT 288. New figure, found in rubble of old House of Images (cf. p. 11.). 10 kg., 40 cm.

HT 288, side.

580

581

HT 289. Female. R.h. held cutlass to r. shoulder. New figure, found in rubble of old House of Images. 18 kg., 51 cm.

HT 289, side.

582

583

Repaired Figures

These images are among those which were repaired subsequent to the original numbering and photography in 1965 and early 1966, and hence were not assigned HT numbers.

H 2 - T 44.
18 kg., 60 cm.

584

H 2 - T 44, side.

585

Repaired Figures

unnumbered H-T 487. 13 kg., 50 cm.

586

unnumbered H-T 487, side.

587

H 43 - T 689. 25 kg., 59 cm.

588

H 43 - T 689, side.

589

590

H 46 - T 258. R.h.
holds fly whisk
over r. shoulder.
14 kg., 52 cm.

H 46 - T 258,
side.

591

592

H 77 - T 492.
15 kg., 57 cm.

H 77 - T 492,
side.

593

263

Repaired Figures

594

H 120 - T 378.
R.h. held staff,
down centre.
18 kg., 53 cm.

H 120 - T 378,
side.

595

H 164 - T 239.
Narrow quiver,
but no strap.
24 kg., 66 cm.

596

H 164 - T 239,
side.

597

H 198 - T 485.
14 kg., 51 cm.

H 198 - T 485,
side.

598

599

H 256 -
unnumbered T.
7 kg., 39 cm.

H 256 -
unnumbered T,
side.

600

601

Repaired Figures

602

H 260 - T 326.
15 kg., 54 cm.

H 260 - T 326,
side.

603

604

unnumbered H -
T 682. 19 kg.,
53 cm.

unnumbered H -
T 682, side.

605

H 308 - T 1.
Female. L.h. held
cutlass over
l. shoulder.
16 kg., 55 cm.

606

H 308 - T 1, side.

607

H 315 - T 216.
33 kg., 66 cm.

608

H 315 - T 216,
side.

609

Repaired Figures

610

H 348 - T 95. R.h. holds dagger on lap. 36 kg., 68 cm.

H 348 - T 95, side.

611

612

unnumbered H - T 174. Single braid extended from top of head down over r. temple. 25 kg., 61 cm.

unnumbered H - T 174, side.

613

H 362 - T 660.
14 kg., 51 cm.

614

H 362 - T 660,
side.

615

H 394 - T 238.
Female. 4 r.v.c.
back of neck.
35 kg., 73 cm.

616

H 394 - T 238,
side.

617

Repaired Figures

618

H 424 - T 27. R.h.
held cutlass,
point down.
23 kg., 50 cm.

H 424 - T 27,
side.

619

620

H 431 - T 550.
Ears
asymmetrical.
R.h. was on
chest. 27 kg.,
60 cm.

H 431 - T 550,
side.

621

H 461 - T 510.
39 kg., 72 cm.

622

H 461 - T 510,
side.

623

H 462 - T 442.
Calabash-bottle
motif front of
coiffure. 21 kg.,
60 cm.

624

H 462 - T 442,
side.

625

Repaired Figures

626

627

unnumbered H - T 538. Both hands probably held staff, down centre. 11 kg., 49 cm.

unnumbered H - T 538, side.

628

629

H 480 - T 180. Female. R.h. held cutlass over r. shoulder. 24 kg., 51 cm.

H 480 - T 180, side.

Heads

Classification

As indicated in the Introduction to the Plates, the heads and headed torsos were classified according to styles of coiffure and headgear. Several categories were devised, and the objects within each were classified, in general, along a continuum from plain to decorated or from simple to complex. Following are the broad categories used, and the numbers of the heads that fall within them.

Diagnostic Feature	Object Nos.	Diagnostic Feature	Object Nos.
Conical peaked caps	H 1 - 102	Hair styled in chevron-like motifs	H 304 - 330
Caps with from 4 to 8 sides	H 103 - 130	Hair styled in "bulbs"	
Caps with vertical ridges	H 131 - 140	(see text, p. 59, and fig. V.14)	H 331 - 361
Domed caps	H 141 - 185	Combinations of the above, with	
Fez-like caps	H 186 - 195	long braid from top down to one side	H 362 - 366
Hair styled in vertical loops	H 196 - 243	Variations on "bulbs"	H 367 - 371
Hair styled in flat squares	H 244 - 255	Variations on chevron motifs	H 372 - 418
Hair styled in triangle motifs	H 256 - 278	Hair styled in braids	H 419 - 542
Hair styled in diamond-shaped motifs	H 279 - 297	Miscellaneous	H 543 - 551
Combinations of the above motifs	H 298 - 303		

In the captions, abbreviations and special designations used are the same as those for the HT and T figures, as discussed in the Introduction to the Plates; but here, "back" means the back of the neck, the area just below the occiput.

Heads Not Pictured

Photographs of 163 heads and head fragments listed below have not been included here because of one of the following reasons: (A) the head, though complete, is too abraded to exhibit significant diagnostic features; (B) the object is a fragment of a head, and lacks sufficient diagnostic features to merit its representation; or (C) the head has been joined to a torso, in which case it appears with the Repaired Figures.

H 2, C	H 167, A	H 267, B	H 414, A
3, B	169, B	268, A	421, B
4, B	170, B	270, A	424, C
11, A	172, B	271, A	426, A
16, B	175, B	272, A	427, A
26, B	180, B	274, B	429, A
36, C	182, B	275, B	431, C
43, C	193, B	278, A	432, A
47, A	194, B	279, B	434, A
54, B	195, B	281, B	437, B
58, A	198, C	283, B	441, B
59, A	201, B	286, B	444, B
60, B	207, B	288, A	446, A
61, B	208, B	289, B	452, B
65, A	211, B	296, A	453, A
72, A	212, B	307, B	454, A
74, B	213, A	308, C	456, A
75, B	214, A	311, A	462, C
77, C	217, A	313, B	464, A
79, C	218, B	315, C	475, A
80, B	224, B	319, B	478, A
82, B	226, B	321, B	480, C
86, B	227, B	325, B	483, B
87, B	228, A	332, B	484, B
88, B	230, B	334, B	486, B
90, B	231, B	337, B	489, A
99, B	232, B	338, A	497, B
112, B	233, B	348, C	501, A
113, B	234, B	350, B	510, B
114, B	235, B	354, A	512, A
120, C	236, B	356, B	517, B
127, B	237, B	362, C	520, B
135, A	238, B	363, B	521, B
138, B	239, B	368, A	523, B
145, A	243, B	371, B	526, A
154, B	249, A	374, A	531, A
155, B	250, B	382, A	536, A
156, B	251, B	394, C	539, B
157, B	256, A	404, B	544, B
163, B	258, B	412, A	552, B
164, C	260, C	413, A	

For nearly all of the heads which are pictured, both front and side views are given; when an object is fragmentary, only one view may appear. Unavoidably, the second shot of a head may appear on the subsequent page.

630
H 1. 29 cm.

631
H 1, side.

632
H 5. 28 cm.

633
H 5, side.

634
H 6. 29 cm.

635
H 6, side.

636
H 7. 16 cm.

637
H 7, side.

638
H 8. 27 cm.

639
H 8, side.

640
H 9. Upper & lower teeth
protrude. 24 cm.

641
H 9, side.

642
H 10. 19 cm.

643
H 10, side.

644
H 12. 23.5 cm.

645
H 12, side.

646
H 13. Tongue protrudes.
30 cm.

647
H 13, side.

648
H 14. 3 r.v.c. back. 27 cm.

649
H 14, side.

650
H 15. 26.5 cm.

651
H 15, side.

652
H 17. 19.5 cm.

653
H 17, side.

654
H 18. 23 cm.

655
H 19. 27 cm.

656
H 20. 22 cm.

657
H 21. Back of neck squared.
4 r.v.c. back. 24 cm.

H 21-25, 27, 28

658
H 21, side.

659
H 22. 27 cm.

660
H 23. Holes in nostrils and ears. Cheekbones sculpted. 22 cm.

661
H 23, side.

662
H 24. Teeth protrude. 21.5 cm.

663
H 24, side.

664
H 25. 19 cm.

665
H 25, side.

666
H 27. 24 cm.

667
H 27, side.

668
H 28. 17 cm.

669
H 28, side.

670
H 29. 24.5 cm.

671
H 29, side.

672
H 30. Upper teeth visible.
35 cm.

673
H 30, side.

674
H 31. 26.5 cm.

675
H 31, side.

676
H 32. Light, porous stone.
29 cm.

677
H 32, side.

678
H 33. 35 cm.

679
H 33, side.

680
H 34. Female? 40.5 cm.

681
H 34, side.

682
H 35. Back of head is H 36.
21.5 cm.

683
H 37. Calabash-bottle motif
on cap. 21.5 cm.

684
H 37, side.

685
H 38. 21 cm.

686
H 38, side.

687
H 39. With frag. back of
head. 29 cm.

688
H 39, side.

689
H 40. 5 r.v.c. back. 32 cm.

690
H 40, side.

691
H 41. 29.5 cm.

692
H 41, side.

693
H 42. 30.5 cm.

694
H 42, side.

695
H 44. Tongue visible.
22.5 cm.

696
H 44, side.

697
H 45. 3 r.v.c. back. 23 cm.

698
H 45, side.

699
H 46, 3 r.v.c. back. 21 cm.

700
H 46, side.

701
H 48. 23.5 cm.

702
H 48, side.

703
H 49. 23.5 cm.

704
H 49, side.

705
H 50. 24 cm.

706
H 50, side.

707
H 51. 21.5 cm.

708
H 51, side.

709
H 52. 22 cm.

710
H 53. 25 cm.

711
H 53, side.

712
H 55. 37.5 cm.

713
H 55, side.

714
H 56. 26.5 cm.

715
H 56, side.

716
H 57. 18.5 cm.

717
H 57, side.

718
H 62. 29 cm.

719
H 62, side.

720
H 63. 27.5 cm.

721
H 63, side.

722
H 64. 27 cm.

723
H 64, side.

724
H 66. 23 cm.

725
H 66, side.

726
H 67. 20.5 cm.

727
H 67, side.

728
H 68. 22 cm.

729
H 68, side.

730
H 69. 16 cm.

731
H 69, side.

732
H 70. 21.5 cm.

733
H 70, side.

734
H 71. 20 cm.

735
H 73. 24.5 cm.

736
H 73, side.

737
H 76. 21 cm.

738
H 76, side.

739
H 78. 4 r.v.c. back. 25.5 cm.

740
H 78, side.

741
H 81. 20.5 cm.

742
H 83. 20.5 cm.

743
H 83, side.

744
H 84. 23 cm.

745
H 84, side.

746
H 85. 22 cm.

747
H 85, side.

748
H 89. 4 r.v.c. back. 28.5 cm.

749
H 89, side.

750
H 91. 3 r.v.c. back. 20.5 cm.

751
H 91, side.

752
H 92. 4 r.v.c. back. 25.5 cm.

753
H 92, side.

754
H 93. 26.5 cm.

755
H 93, side.

756
H 94. Fingers of l.h. at chin. 25 cm.

757
H 94, side.

758
H 95. 27 cm.

H 95-98, 100-102

759
H 95, side.

760
H 96. 22.5 cm.

761
H 97. 3 r.v.c. back. 28 cm.

762
H 97, side.

763
H 98. 25.5 cm.

764
H 100. 25 cm.

765
H 100, side.

766
H 101. 3 r.v.c. back. 26 cm.

767
H 101, side.

768
H 102. 23 cm.

769
H 102, side.

770
H 103. 20.5 cm.

771
H 103, side.

772
H 104. 25.5 cm.

773
H 104, side.

774
H 105. 24 cm.

775
H 106. 24 cm.

776
H 106, side.

777
H 107. 26.5 cm.

778
H 107, side.

779
H 108. 25 cm.

780
H 108, side.

781
H 109. 26.5 cm.

H 109-111, 115-117

782
H 109, side.

783
H 110. 28 cm.

784
H 110, side.

785
H 111. 19 cm.

786
H 111, side.

787
H 115. 26.5 cm.

788
H 115, side.

789
H 116. 30.5 cm.

790
H 116, side.

791
H 117. 25.5 cm.

792
H 117, side.

793
H 118. 23.5 cm.

794
H 119. 18.5 cm.

795
H 121. 29 cm.

796
H 121, side.

797
H 122. 3 r.v.c. back. 24 cm.

798
H 122, side.

799
H 123. 23.5 cm.

800
H 123, side.

801
H 124. 21.5 cm.

802
H 125. 21 cm.

803
H 125, side.

804
H 126. Possibly complete
as a bust. 24 cm.

H 126, 128-132

805
H 126, side.

806
H 128. Bust. Neck
hollowed to a depth of
6 cm. Ht. 33 cm.

807
H 128, side.

808
H 129. Eating something;
Esiẹ people say a piece of
yam. 20 cm.

809
H 129, side.

810
H 130. 17 cm.

811
H 130, side.

812
H 131. Upper teeth appear
filed. Marks on chin like
HT 58. 34.5 cm.

813
H 131, side.

814
H 132. 25.5 cm.

815
H 132, side.

816
H 133. 6 teeth, apparently
filed. 19.5 cm.

817
H 133, side.

818
H 134. 25.5 cm.

819
H 134, side.

820
H 136. 4 r.v.c. back of neck.
28 cm.

821
H 136, side.

822
H 137. With frag. back of
head. 26 cm.

823
H 139. 25 cm.

293

824
H 139, side.

825
H 140. 21 cm.

826
H 140, side.

827
H 141. 21 cm.

828
H 141, side.

829
H 142. 25 cm.

830
H 142, side.

831
H 143. 5 teeth, apparently filed. 18 cm.

832
H 143, side.

833
H 144. 14.5 cm.

834
H 144, side.

835
H 146. 23.5 cm.

836
H 146, side.

837
H 147. 19 cm.

838
H 147, side.

839
H 148. Tongue protrudes.
15 cm.

840
H 148, side.

841
H 149. 25.5 cm.

842
H 149, side.

843
H 150. 23.5 cm.

844
H 150, side.

845
H 151. 20 cm.

846
H 151, side.

847
H 152. 20 cm.

H 152, 153, 158-161

848
H 152, side.

849
H 153. 3 r.v.c. back. 29 cm.

850
H 153, side.

851
H 158. 3 r.v.c. back.
27.5 cm.

852
H 158, side.

853
H 159. 4 r.v.c. back. 23 cm.

854
H 159, side.

855
H 160. 4 r.v.c. back.

856
H 160, side.

857
H 161. 22 cm.

858
H 161, side.

859
H 162. 26 cm.

860
H 162, side.

861
H 165. 24.5 cm.

862
H 165, side.

863
H 166. 25.5 cm.

864
H 166, side.

865
H 168. 17 cm.

866
H 168, side.

867
H 171. 23 cm.

868
H 171, side.

869
H 173. 3 r.v.c. back.
25.5 cm.

870
H 173, side.

871
H 174. 24 cm.

872
H 174, side.

873
H 176. Calabash-bottle
motif front of cap. 20 cm.

874
H 176, side.

875
H 177. 21.5 cm.

876
H 177, side.

877
H 178. 28 cm.

878
H 178, side.

879
H 179. 37.5 cm.

880
H 181. 17.5 cm.

881
H 181, side.

882
H 183. 20 cm.

883
H 183, side.

884
H 184. 26.5 cm.

885
H 185. 23 cm.

886
H 185, side.

887
H 186. 21 cm.

H 186-191

888
H 186, side.

889
H 187. 19.5 cm.

890
H 187, side.

891
H 188. 17 cm.

892
H 188, side.

893
H 189. 24 cm.

894
H 189, side.

895
H 190. 28 cm.

896
H 190, side.

897
H 191. 35.5 cm.

898
H 191, side.

899
H 192. 21 cm.

900
H 192, side.

901
H 196. 20 cm.

902
H 196, side.

903
H 197. 19 cm.

904
H 197, side.

905
H 199. 21 cm.

906
H 199, side.

907
H 200. 18.5 cm.

908
H 200, side.

909
H 202. 21.5 cm.

910
H 202, side.

911
H 203. 16 cm.

912
H 203, side.

913
H 204. 18.5 cm.

914
H 204, side.

915
H 205. 23 cm.

916
H 205, side.

917
H 206. 19 cm.

918
H 206, side.

919
H 209. 26.5 cm.

920
H 209, side.

921
H 210. 25.5 cm.

922
H 210, side.

923
H 215. 3 r.v.c. back. 24 cm.

924
H 216. 21.5 cm.

925
H 216, side.

926
H 219. 21.5 cm.

927
H 219, side.

H 220-223, 225, 229, 240

928
H 220. 23 cm.

929
H 220, side.

930
H 221. 32.5 cm.

931
H 221, side.

932
H 222. 2 visible r.v.c. back.
19.5 cm.

933
H 222, side.

934
H 223. 4 r.v.c. back. 12 cm.

935
H 223, side.

936
H 225. 24 cm.

937
H 229. 19.5 cm.

938
H 229, side.

939
H 240. 21.5 cm.

940
H 240, side.

941
H 241. 19.5 cm.

942
H 241, side.

943
H 242. 22 cm.

944
H 244. Complete as head.
18.5 cm.

945
H 244, side.

946
H 245. Complete as head;
see text, pp. 63-4. 22 cm.

947
H 245, side.

948
H 246. 3 r.v.c. back.
21.5 cm.

949
H 246, side.

950
H 247. 4 r.v.c. back.
21.5 cm.

951
H 247, side.

952
H 248. 16.5 cm.

953
H 248, side.

954
H 252. With frag. back of head. 22 cm.

955
H 253. 3 calabash-bottle motifs top of coiffure. 3 r.v.c. back. 17 cm.

956
H 253, side.

957
H 254. 3 r.v.c. back. 24.5 cm.

958
H 254, side.

959

H 255. 3 r.v.c. back. See text. p. 63. 24 cm.

960

H 255, side.

961

H 257. 3 r.v.c. back. 20 cm.

962

H 257, side.

963

H 259. Beaded and tasseled band hangs from coiffure. 16 cm.

964

H 259, side.

965

H 261. 3 r.v.c. back. 20 cm.

966

H 262. With frag. back of head. Raised square cic. back. 19 cm.

967

H 262, side.

H 263-266, 269

968

H 263. With frag. back of
head. 19.5 cm.

969

H 263, side.

970

H 264. 18 cm.

971

H 264, side.

972

H 265. 3 r.v.c. back.
18.5 cm.

973

H 265, side.

974

H 266. 20 cm.

975

H 266, side.

976

H 269. 2 frags. 23 cm.

977

H 273. Frag. back of head discovered later; has large calabash-bottle motif on coiffure. 21.5 cm.

978

H 273, side.

979

H 276. 3 r.v.c. back.

980

H 276, side.

981

H 277. 20 cm.

982

H 277, side.

983

H 280. With frag. l. side of coiffure. 19 cm.

984

H 280, side.

985

H 282. 16.5 cm.

986

H 284. 4 r.v.c. back. See text, p. 63, 19 cm.

987
H 284, side.

988
H 285. 33.5 cm.

989
H 285, side.

990
H 287. 3 r.v.c. back. 18 cm.

991
H 287, side.

992
H 290. 20 cm.

993
H 290, side.

994
H 291. 3 r.v.c. back. 20 cm.

995
H 291, side.

996
H 292. 3 r.v.c. back.
Fingertips in mouth?
20 cm.

997
H 292, side.

998
H 293. 3 r.v.c. back. Frag.
top of head discovered
later. 16.5 cm.

999
H 293, side.

1,000
H 294. 3 r.v.c. back.
16.5 cm.

1,001
H 294, side.

1,002
H 295. 20 cm.

1,003
H 295, side.

H 297-301

1,004

H 297. 3 r.v.c. back. 15 cm.

1,005

H 297, side.

1,006

H 298. 3 r.v.c. back.
21.5 cm.

1,007

H 298, side.

1,008

H 299. 3 r.v.c. back.
25.5 cm.

1,009

H 299, side.

1,010

H 300. 19 cm.

1,011

H 300, side.

1,012

H 301. Frag. r. side of head
discovered later. 20 cm.

1,013

H 301, side.

1,014
H 302. 26 cm.

1,015
H 302, side.

1,016
H 303. 3 r.v.c. back. 21 cm.

1,017
H 303, side.

1,018
H 304. 4 r.v.c. back. 19 cm.

1,019
H 304, side.

1,020
H 305. 21.5 cm.

1,021
H 305, side.

1,022
H 306. 20 cm.

1,023
H 306, side.

1,024
H 309. Female. 3 r.v.c.
back. Cic. down back, sim.
to HT 181. 37 cm.

1,025
H 309, side.

H 310, 312, 314, 316, 317

1,026
H 310. 3 r.v.c. back. See
text, p. 63. 18.5 cm.

1,027
H 310, side.

1,028
H 312. 19.5 cm.

1,029
H 312, side.

1,030
H 314. 22 cm.

1,031
H 314, side.

1,032
H 316. 24.5 cm.

1,033
H 316, side.

1,034
H 317. 3 r.v.c. back.
17.5 cm.

1,035
H 317, side.

1,036
H 318. 3 r.v.c. back. 20 cm.

1,037
H 318, side.

1,038
H 320. 3 r.v.c. back. 21 cm.

1,039
H 320, side.

1,040
H 322. 22 cm.

1,041
H 322, side.

1,042
H 323. 3 r.v.c.
back. 19.5 cm.

1,043
H 323, side.

1,044
H 324. 3 r.v.c.
back. 21.5 cm.

1,045
H 324, side.

1,046
H 326. 23.5 cm.

1,047
H 326, side.

1,048
H 327. 3 r.v.c.
back. 16 cm.

1,049
H 327, side.

1,050
H 328. 17.5 cm.

1,051
H 328, side.

1,052
H 329. 3 r.v.c.
back. 24 cm.

1,053
H 329, side.

1,054
H 330. 3 r.v.c.
back. 22 cm.

1,055
H 330, side.

1,056
H 331. 23 cm.

1,057
H 331, side.

1,058
H 333. 23.5 cm.

1,059
H 333, side.

1,060
H 335. Large calabash-bottle motif top of coiffure. 21 cm.

1,061
H 335, side.

1,062
H 336. 17 cm.

1,063
H 336, side.

1,064
H 339. 23 cm.

1,065
H 339, side.

1,066
H 340. 2 frags. 28 cm.

1,067
H 341. Top of head quite flat. 20 cm.

1,068
H 341, side.

1,069
H 342. 24 cm.

1,070
H 343. 4 r.v.c.
back. 20 cm.

1,071
H 343, side.

1,072
H 344. 3 r.v.c.
back. 28 cm.

1,073
H 344, side.

1,074
H 345. 3 r.v.c.
back. 20 cm.

1,075
H 345, side.

1,076
H 346. 22 cm.

1,077
H 346, side.

1,078
H 347. 3 r.v.c.
back. 23 cm.

1,079
H 347, side.

1,080
H 349. 24 cm.

1,081
H 349, side.

1,082
H 351. 3 r.v.c. back.
Calabash-bottle motif top
25.5 cm.

1,083
H 351, side.

1,084
H 352. 20 cm.

1,085
H 352, side.

1,086
H 353. 24 cm.

1,087
H 353, side.

1,088
H 355. 21.5 cm.

1,089
H 355, side.

H 357-361, 364

1,090
H 357. 3 r.v.c.
back. 22 cm.

1,091
H 358. 3 r.v.c.
back. 21.5 cm.

1,092
H 358, side.

1,093
H 359. 4 r.v.c.
back. 29 cm.

1,094
H 359, side.

1,095
H 360. 23 cm.

1,096
H 360, side.

1,097
H 361. 3 r.v.c.
back. 23 cm.

1,098
H 361, side.

1,099
H 364. 3 r.v.c.
back. 21 cm.

1,100
H 364, side.

1,101
H 365. 21 cm.

1,102
H 365, side.

1,103
H 366. Large braid from top
nearly to l. ear. 17 cm.

1,104
H 366, side.

1,105
H 367. 23.5 cm.

1,106
H 367, side.

1,107
H 369. Prominent
cheekbones and forehead.
23.5 cm.

1,108
H 369, side.

1,109
H 370. Head on solid
pedestal. 33 cm.

1,110
H 370, side.

1,111
H 372. 19 cm.

1,112
H 372, side.

1,113
H 373. 20 cm.

1,114
H 373, side.

1,115
H 375. The only head
shorter than 15 cm. still
remaining in the collection
(see text, p. 9). 10 cm.

1,116
H 375, side.

1,117
H 376. 3 r.v.c.
back. 16.5 cm.

1,118
H 376, side.

1,119
H 377. 17.5 cm.

1,120
H 377, side.

1,121
H 378. 20 cm.

1,122
H 378, side.

1,123
H 379. 19 cm.

1,124
H 379, side.

1,125
H 380. 18.5 cm.

1,126
H 380, side.

1,127
H 381. 21.5 cm.

1,128
H 381, side.

1,129
H 383. 3 r.v.c.
back. 19 cm.

1,130
H 383, side.

1,131
H 384. 3 r.v.c. back. Worn
calabash-bottle motif centre
coiffure. 21.5 cm.

1,132
H 384, side.

1,133
H 385. 22 cm.

1,134
H 385, side.

1,135
H 386. 20 cm.

1,136
H 386, side.

1,137
H 387. 3 r.v.c.
back. 20 cm.

1,138
H 387, side.

1,139
H 388. 3 r.v.c.
back. 21 cm.

1,140
H 388, side.

1,141
H 389. 20 cm.

1,142
H 389, side.

1,143
H 390. 21 cm.

1,144
H 390, side.

1,145
H 391. 3 r.v.c.
back. 23.5 cm.

1,146
H 391, side.

1,147
H 392. 18.5 cm.

1,148
H 392, side.

1,149
H 393. 18.5 cm.

1,150
H 393, side.

1,151
H 395. 21.5 cm.

1,152
H 395, side.

1,153
H 396. 21 cm.

1,154
H 396, side.

1,155
H 397. Front of face
smashed. 32.5 cm.

1,156
H 398. L. side broken off.
20 cm.

1,157
H 399. 19 cm.

1,158
H 399, side.

1,159
H 400. 23 cm.

1,160
H 400, side.

1,161
H 401. 21 cm.

1,162
H 401, side.

1,163
H 402. 3 r.v.c.
back. 38 cm.

1,164
H 402, side.

1,165
H 403. Mounted on plaster
block prior to 1965. 29 cm.

1,166
H 403, side.

1,167
H 405. 27 cm.

1,168
H 405, side.

1,169
H 406. 25 cm.

1,170
H 406, side.

1,171
H 407. 23 cm.

1,172
H 407, side.

1,173
H 408. 20 cm.

1,174
H 408, side.

1,175
H 409. R.h. on r.
cheek. 21 cm.

1,176
H 409, side.

1,177
H 410. 4 r.v.c.
back. 21 cm.

1,178
H 410, side.

1,179
H 411. 4 r.v.c.
back. 23 cm.

1,180
H 411, side.

1,181

H 415. 3 r.v.c.
back. 24 cm.

1,182

H 415, side.

1,183

H 416. 3 r.v.c.
back. 23 cm.

1,184

H 416, side.

1,185

H 417. 22 cm.

1,186

H 418. 22 cm.

1,187

H 418, side.

1,188

H 419. 19.5 cm.

1,189

H 419, side.

1,190

H 420. 3 r.v.c.
back. 20 cm.

1,191

H 420, side.

1,192
H 422. 23 cm.

1,193
H 422, side.

1,194
H 423. 19 cm.

1,195
H 423, side.

1,196
H 425. 19 cm.

1,197
H 425, side.

1,198
H 428. 3 r.v.c.
back. 15 cm.

1,199
H 428, side.

1,200
H 430. Female. 3 r.v.c.
back. 33 cm.

1,201
H 430, side.

1,202
H 433. 21 cm.

1,203
H 433, side.

H 435, 436, 438-440, 442

1,204

H 435. 3 r.v.c.
back. 22 cm.

1,205

H 435, side.

1,206

H 436. 21 cm.

1,207

H 436, side.

1,208

H 438. 31 cm.

1,209

H 438, side.

1,210

H 439. 24 cm.

1,211

H 439, side.

1,212

H 440. 29 cm.

1,213

H 440, side.

1,214

H 442. Chin to occiput,
18.5 cm. Ht. 15 cm.

1,215
H 442, side.

1,216
H 443. 21 cm.

1,217
H 443, side.

1,218
H 445. 4 r.v.c.
back. 25 cm.

1,219
H 445, side.

1,220
H 447. 3 r.v.c.
back. 23 cm.

1,221
H 447, side.

1,222
H 448. 20.5 cm.

1,223
H 448, side.

1,224
H 449. 17 cm.

1,225
H 449, side.

1,226

H 450. 3 r.v.c.
back.

1,227

H 450, side.

1,228

H 451. 36.5 cm.

1,229

H 451, side.

1,230

H 455. 25 cm.

1,231

H 445, side.

1,232

H 457. 3 r.v.c.
back. 22.5 cm.

1,233

H 457, side.

1,234

H 458. 19 cm.

1,235

H 458, side.

1,236

H 459. 23 cm.

1,237

H 459, side.

1,238
H 460. 20 cm.

1,239
H 460, side.

1,240
H 461. 24 cm.

1,241
H 461, side.

1,242
H 463. 25 cm.

1,243
H 463, side.

1,244
H 465. 21 cm.

1,245
H 465, side.

1,246
H 466. With frag. back of
head. 26 cm.

1,247
H 467. 4 r.v.c.
back. 25 cm.

1,248
H 467, side.

1,249
H 468. 23 cm.

1,250
H 468, side.

1,251
H 469. 3 r.v.c.
back. 25 cm.

1,252
H 469, side.

1,253
H 470. 4 r.v.c.
back. 25 cm.

1,254
H 470, side.

1,255
H 471. 3 r.v.c. back.
Necklace tie like HT 108.
33 cm.

1,256
H 471, side.

1,257
H 472. 17 cm.

1,258
H 472, side.

1,259
H 473. 19 cm.

1,260
H 473, side.

1,261
H 474. 4 r.v.c.
back. 21 cm.

1,262
H 474, side.

1,263
H 476. 19 cm.

1,264
H 476, side.

1,265
H 477. 4 r.v.c.
back. 22 cm.

1,266
H 477, side.

1,267
H 479. 4 r.v.c.
back. 18 cm.

1,268
H 479, side.

1,269
H 481. 19 cm.

1,270
H 481, side.

1,271
H 482. 3 r.v.c. back. Large
calabash-bottle motif top.
22 cm.

1,272
H 482, side.

335

H 485, 487, 488, 490-492

1,273
H 485. 4 r.v.c.
back. 21 cm.

1,274
H 485, side.

1,275
H 487. 23 cm.

1,276
H 487, side.

1,277
H 488. 20 cm.

1,278
H 488, side.

1,279
H 490. 3 r.v.c.
back. 13 cm.

1,280
H 490, side.

1,281
H 491. Calabash-bottle
motif forehead. 22 cm.

1,282
H 491, side.

1,283
H 492. 22 cm.

1,284
H 492, side.

1,285
H 493. 22 cm.

1,286
H 493, side.

1,287
H 494. 4 r.v.c.
back. 20 cm.

1,288
H 494, side.

1,289
H 495. Calabash-bottle
motif top. 22.5 cm.

1,290
H 495, side.

1,291
H 496. 21 cm.

1,292
H 496, side.

1,293
H 498. 27 cm.

1,294
H 498, side.

1,295
H 499. 20 cm.

1,296
H 499, side.

1,297
H 500. 18 cm.

1,298
H 500, side.

1,299
H 502. 24 cm.

1,300
H 502, side.

1,301
H 503. 20 cm.

1,302
H 503, side.

1,303
H 504. 23 cm.

1,304
H 504, side.

1,305
H 505. 3 r.v.c. back.
Calabash-bottle motif top.
23 cm.

1,306
H 505, side.

1,307
H 506. Calabash-bottle
motif front and back of
coiffure. 21 cm.

1,308
H 506, side.

1,309
H 507. 19 cm.

1,310
H 507, side.

1,311
H 508. 3 r.v.c.
back. 21.5 cm.

1,312
H 508, side.

1,313
H 509. Female.
32 cm.

1,314
H 509, side.

1,315
H 511. 3 r.v.c.
back. 16 cm.

1,316
H 511, side.

1,317
H 513. 3 r.v.c.
back. 24.5 cm.

1,318
H 513, side.

1,319
H 514. 3 r.v.c.
back. 21 cm.

1,320
H 514, side.

1,321

H 515. 3 r.v.c.
back. 24 cm.

1,322

H 515, side.

1,323

H 516. 27 cm.

1,324

H 516, side.

1,325

H 518. 18 cm.

1,326

H 518, side.

1,327

H 519. 3 r.v.c.
back.

1,328

H 519, side.

1,329

H 522. 3 r.v.c.
back. 21 cm.

1,330

H 522, side.

1,331

H 524. 3 r.v.c.
back. 23 cm.

1,332

H 524, side.

1,333

H 525. 23 cm.

1,334

H 525, side.

1,335

H 527. 3 r.v.c.
back. 17 cm.

1,336

H 527, side.

1,337

H 528. 26 cm.

1,338

H 528, side.

1,339

H 529. 21 cm.

1,340

H 529, side.

1,341

H 530. Calabash -bottle
motif forehead. 26.5 cm.

1,342

H 530, side.

1,343

H 532. 18.5 cm.

1,344

H 532, side.

H 533-535, 537, 538, 540

1,345

H 533. 24.5 cm.

1,346

H 533, side.

1,347

H 534. 22.5 cm.

1,348

H 534, side.

1,349

H 535. 25.5 cm.

1,350

H 535, side.

1,351

H 537. 20.5 cm.

1,352

H 537, side.

1,353

H 538. 18 cm.

1,354

H 538, side.

1,355

H 540. 3 r.v.c.
back.

1,356

H 540, side.

1,357

H 541. 3 r.v.c.
back.

1,358

H 541, side.

1,359

H 542. 25 cm.

1,360

H 542, side.

1,361

H 543. 21 cm.

1,362

H 543, side.

1,363

H 545. 2 frags. poorly
joined with cement prior to
1965. Complete as head;
flat back like H 245, but
with small hole as if for
hanging from a peg. 17 cm.

1,364

H 545, side.

1,365

H 546. Complete as head.
See text, pp. 53-4, 61.
29 cm.

1,366

H 546, l. side.

1,367

H 546, r. side.

H 547-551
Heads Discovered After Original Cataloguing

1,368

H 547. 21.5 cm.

1,369

H 547, side.

1,370

H 548. Female. Cutlass
point to r. shoulder. 35 cm.

1,371

H 548, side.

1,372

H 549. 3 r.v.c.
back. 34 cm.

1,373

H 550. 23 cm.

1,374

H 550, side.

1,375

H 551. 28.5 cm.

1,376

H 551, side.

1,377

Unnumbered (A). Found in rubble of old House of Images. 21.5 cm.

1,378

Unnumbered (A), side.

1,379

Unnumbered (B). Found in rubble of old House of Images. 20 cm.

1,380

Unnumbered (B), side.

1,381

Unnumbered (C). Found in rubble of old House of Images. 24 cm.

1,382

Unnumbered (C), side.

1,383

Head stolen from collection, recovered and presented to the National Museum, Lagos, in 1949 (cat. no. 49.24.1).

1,384

Side of National Museum head.

Torsos

Weights are recorded for those torsos re-photographed in 1974 (black background).

T 2. 51 kg.,
71 cm.

1,385

T 5. Female.
48 cm.

1,386

T 7, 11, 14, 15

T 7. Female.
40 cm.

T 11. Cic. down
back; bare
buttocks. 16 kg.,
44 cm.

1,387

1,388

T 14. Female.
Cic. down back.
30 kg., 45 cm.

T 15. Female.
Holding kola nut
pod. 34 cm.

1,389

1,390

T 16. Female. 36 cm.

1,391

T 18. 49 cm.

1,392

T 19. 52 kg., 66 cm.

1,393

T 20. Female. 51 cm.

1,394

T 21. 33 kg.,
55 cm.

1,395

T 24. 14 kg.,
36 cm.

1,396

T 25. 14 kg.,
42 cm.

1,397

T 26. 37 cm.

1,398

T 29. Female. 49 cm.

1,399

T 31. Female. 43 cm.

1,400

T 33. Cic. down back. 45 cm.

1,401

T 34. Female. 15 kg., 54 cm.

1,402

T 35. Female? Fly whisk over r. shoulder. 40 cm.

1,403

T 40. 14 kg., 36 cm.

1,404

T 41. 18 kg., 37 cm.

1,405

T 43, 41 cm.

1,406

T 46. Female.
53 cm.

1,407

T 47. 24 kg.,
49 cm.

1,408

T 48. Sheathed
dagger rear.
50 cm.

1,409

T 51. 41 cm.

1,410

T 53, 55-57

1,411

T 53. Sheathed dagger rear. 46 cm.

T 55. 43 cm.

1,412

T 56. 50 cm.

1,413

T 57. Female. Cic. down back. 27 kg., 50 cm.

1,414

T 58. Female. 27 kg., 43 cm.

1,415

T 65. 15 kg., 38 cm.

1,416

T 67. Female. 26 kg., 42 cm.

1,417

T 67, rear.

1,418

T 70, 73, 76, 77

T 70. Female.
22 kg., 43 cm.

1,419

T 73. 10 kg.,
35 cm.

1,420

T 76. 40 cm.

1,421

T 77. Sheathed
dagger l. side.
48 cm.

1,422

T 78. Female.
Cic. down back.
14 kg., 35 cm.

1,423

T 80. Female.
Cic. down back.
Kola nut pod on
lap. 17 kg.,
32 cm.

1,424

T 82. 48 cm.

1,425

T 83. 33 kg.,
46 cm.

1,426

T 91, 92, 94

1,427

T 91. 41 kg.,
42 cm.

T 92. 9 kg.,
37 cm.

1,428

T 92, rear.

1,429

T 94. 28 kg.,
45 cm.

1,430

T 96. Cic. down back. 19 kg., 39 cm.

1,431

T101. Drum (Yoruba, àgèrè, a hunter's drum) on lap. 23 kg., 51 cm.

1,432

T 102. Broad knife l. side. 37 kg., 51 cm.

1,433

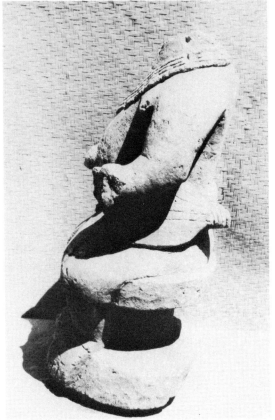

T 102, side.

1,434

T 104-106

T 104. 29 kg., 54 cm.

1,435

T 105. 26 kg., 48 cm.

1,436

T 106. Female. Cic. down back. 42 cm.

1,437

360

T 109. 17 kg.,
39 cm.

1,438

T 109, rear.

1,439

T 116. 32 kg.,
48 cm.

1,440

T 117. 26 kg.,
49 cm.

1,441

T 121, 122, 124

1,442

T 121. 55 cm.

T 121, side.

1,443

T 122. Female.
Cic. down back.
26 kg., 50 cm.

1,444

T 124. Female.
42 kg., 57 cm.

1,445

T 125. 52 cm.

1,446

T 126. 35 kg.,
49 cm.

1,447

T 131. Female.
51 cm.

1,448

T 131, side.

1,449

363

T 134, 136, 139

T 134. 12 kg., 34 cm.

1,450

T 136. Standing. 14 kg., 38 cm.

1,451

T 139. Standing. 14 kg., 34 cm.

1,452

T 140. 55 kg., 64 cm.

1,453

T 140, side.

1,454

T 141. Cic. down back. Bare buttocks. 14 kg., 40 cm.

1,455

T 141, side.

1,456

T 144. Female.
43 kg., 60 cm.

1,457

T 144, rear.

1,458

T 146. 34 kg.,
50 cm.

1,459

T 147. Female.
20 kg., 44 cm.

1,460

T 148. 18 kg.,
42 cm.

1,461

T 148, rear.

1,462

T 151. 25 kg.,
47 cm.

1,463

T 151, rear.

1,464

T 152, 155, 157, 158

T 152. Female.
28 kg., 48 cm.

1,465

T 155. 21 kg.,
43 cm.

1,466

T 157. 51 kg.,
62 cm.

1,467

T 158. 5 kg.,
25 cm.

1,468

T 159. 2.7 kg.,
27 cm.

1,469

T 160. Female.
5 kg., 27 cm.

1,470

T 161. 7 kg.,
29 cm.

1,471

T 162. 27 cm.

1,472

T 163, 167, 171, 175

T 163. 2.7 kg., 26 cm.

1,473

T 167. 14 kg., 31 cm.

1,474

T 171. Cic. down back. 31 kg. No measurement.

1,475

T 175. Dagger and unident. obj. on lap. 19 kg., 47 cm.

1,476

T 177. 43 kg.,
66 cm.

1,477

T 178. Dagger l.
side. 29 kg.,
44 cm.

1,478

T 181. 2 kg.,
25 cm.

1,479

T 185. Cic. down
back. 34 kg.,
58 cm.

1,480

T 190, 192, 198, 202

T 190. 22 kg., 45 cm.

1,481

T 192. Female. 26 kg., 39 cm.

1,482

T 198. Standing. 50 cm.

1,483

T 202. 23 kg., 66 cm.

1,484

T 209. Female?
49 cm.

1,485

T 212. Female.
Cic. down back.
50 cm.

1,486

T 213. Female.
Cic. down back.
49 cm.

1,487

T 218. 55 cm.

1,488

T 224, 227, 230

1,489

T 224. Female. 23 kg., 41 cm.

T 227. 46 cm.

1,490

1,491

T 230. Cic. down back. 61 cm.

T 231. 46 cm.

1,492

T 231, rear.

1,493

T 232. 52 cm.

1,494

T 232, rear.

1,495

T 233. 37 cm.

T 234. Female.
33 cm.

1,496

1,497

T 235. Female.
54 cm.

1,498

T 244. 50 cm.

1,499

T 246. 23 kg.,
43 cm.

1,500

T 250. 49 cm.

1,501

T 251. Female.
39 cm.

1,502

T 259. Braided
beard. 33 kg.,
58 cm.

1,503

T 273, 302, 316, 317

T 273. 27 kg., 52 cm.

1,504

T 302. Showing detail of bow. 28 cm.

1,505

T 316. Matched with T 646. 14 kg., 32 cm.

1,506

T 317. Kneeling, holding kola nut pod. 21 cm.

1,507

378

T 324. Female.
Kneeling, naked,
presenting
tied bundle.
10 kg., 31 cm.

1,508

T 344. Female.
45 cm.

1,509

T 348. 26 kg.,
52 cm.

1,510

T 349. 24 kg.,
40 cm.

1,511

T 350, 361, 364, 367

1,512

T 350. 31 kg., 45 cm.

T 361. 42 cm.

1,513

1,514

T 364. Cic. down back. 23 kg., 48 cm.

T 367. Female. 50 cm.

1,515

T 376. Female.
28 cm.

1,516

T 381. 29 kg.,
40 cm.

1,517

T 392. Incised
spine. 14 kg.,
35 cm.

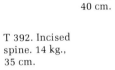

1,518

T 407. Female?
45 cm.

1,519

T 409, 418, 421, 423

T 409. Female. 16 kg., 37 cm.

1,520

T 418. Female. 15 kg., 30 cm.

1,521

1,522

T 421. Bare buttocks. 22 kg., 48 cm.

T 423. Female. 39 kg., 50 cm.

1,523

T 428. Female?
63 cm.

1,524

T 430. Female.
54 cm.

1,525

T 439. Cic. down
back. 15 kg.,
28 cm.

1,526

T 449. 44 cm.

1,527

T 450, 458, 463

1,528

T 450. 24 kg.,
39 cm.

T 458. See text,
pp. 59, 80-1.
35 cm.

1,529

T 458, side.

1,530

T 463. Female.
23 kg., 38 cm.

1,531

T 473. Incised shoulder blades. 35 cm.

1,532

T 476. Female? R.h. held staff. Pubic hair designated by cross-hatching; see text, p. 65. 7 kg., 34 cm.

1,533

T 476, rear.

1,534

T 478. Female. 4 kg., 34 cm.

1,535

T 479, 480

1,536

1,537

1,538

1,539

T 481. 37 cm.

T 481, rear,
showing quiver
and bow.

1,540

1,541

T 482. 45 cm.

T 482, rear.

1,542

1,543

T 487, 491, 503

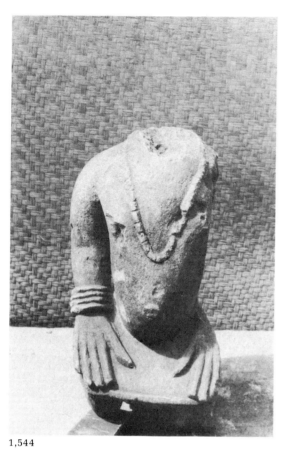

T 487. No measurement.

1,544

T 491. Holding what may be a percussion-type musical instrument, consisting of a gong and striking-tool. 34 cm.

1,545

T 503. 32 cm.

1,546

T 503, rear.

1,547

T 504. 44 kg.,
53 cm.

1,548

T 504, rear.

1,549

T 505. 29 kg.,
49 cm.

1,550

T 506. 35 kg.,
56 cm.

1,551

T 516, 530, 532

T 516. Female.
25 kg., 46 cm.

T 530. 43 cm.

T 530, rear.

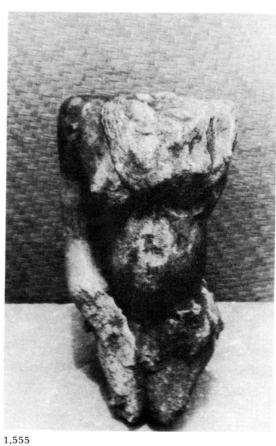

T 532. Female,
kneeling. 31 cm.

T 541. Holding shield. 19 kg., 35 cm.

1,556

T 618. Female. 41 cm.

1,557

T 618, rear.

1,558

T 647, 649, 652

1,559

T 647. Holds fly
whisk over r.
shoulder.
15 kg., 28 cm.

T 647, rear.

1,560

T 649. Female.
41 cm.

1,561

T 652. Female.
Matched with
T 658. 13 kg.,
50 cm.

1,562

T 748. Female. Probably pregnant. 21 cm.

1,563

T 748, rear.

1,564

T 790. The smallest image. Standing. 1.4 kg., 14 cm.

1,565

393

T 801

1,566

T 801. Female.
Pregnant, naked,
string girdle
around hips.
4 kg., 22 cm.

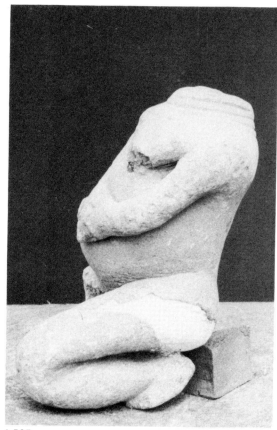

T 801, side.

1,567

Selected Miscellaneous Objects

1,568

M 1. Dog. Length, 27 cm.

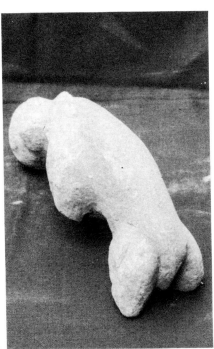

M 1, rear view.

1,569

M 2. Fowl, called àparò (the Senegambian francolin, *Francolinus Bicalartus B.*) by Ẹsiẹ people. Length, 21 cm.

1,570

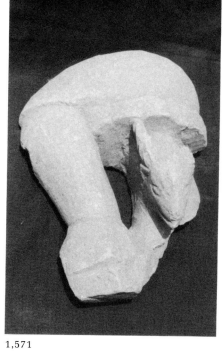

M 3. Fragment of stool with goat beneath. Ht., 26 cm.

1,571

M 4. Spear point. This is the only evidence that spears were a part of the Ẹsiẹ armament.

1,572

M 5. Showing the manner in which some bows were represented. It is significant that when the images were vandalized (cf. text, p. 83), care was taken to destroy weapons; none of the figures with HT or T numbers holds a complete bow.

1,573

M 6. Shield, held
apart from the
image.

M 6, inside of
shield.

1,574

1,575

M 7 (l.), M 8.
Right hands
holding staffs.

M 9. Left hand
holding staff with
bovine head in
relief.

1,576

1,577

M 10. Two hands holding staff.

1,578

M 11. Fragment of upper left arm and elbow. The animal carved in relief is probably a large insect.

1,579

M 12. Arm fragment with calabash-bottle.

M 13, M 14. Calabashes of the type used for palm wine; see text, p. 57. A snake is coiled around M 14 (r.), and a left hand lies flat on the top; but neither object was part of a larger statue. Ht. of each, 26 cm.

1,581

1,580

Ebọra rere mà lère o
Ère gbé wa yún, ere gbé wa bọ̀
Ebọra rere mà lère

Nígbà yí ère kè jà
Kí lòkè nṣe?
Kí lodò nwò?

Ebọra rere mà lère.

The gods which are good are the images
The images protect our going,
    the images protect our coming
The gods which are good are the images.

When the images do not quarrel,
What is the hill doing?
What is the river looking at?

The gods which are good are the images.

Ere Elesie ebora die ko
E yawa wo ere; ere njo.

The images of the Elesie are no small gods
Come and see the images; the images
    are dancing.